SO-AMO-569

Mirko Galli - Claudia Mühlhoff

Virtual Terragni

CAAD in Historical and Critical Research

Preface by Antonino Saggio

Birkhäuser – Publishers for Architecture
Basel • Boston • Berlin

Translation from Italian into English: Lucinda Byatt, Edinburgh

A CIP catalogue record for this book is available from the Library of Congress, Washington D.C., USA.

Deutsche Bibliothek Cataloging-in-Publication Data

Galli, Mirko:
Virtual terragni : CAAD in historical and critical research / Mirko Galli/Claudia Mühlhoff. Foreword by Antonino Saggio. [Transl. into Engl.: Lucinda Byatt]. - Basel ; Boston ; Berlin : Birkhäuser, 2000
  (The IT revolution in architecture)
  Einheitssacht.: Terragni virtuale <engl.>
  ISBN 3-7643-6174-3
  ISBN 0-8176-6174-3

Original edition:
Terragni virtuale (Universale di Architettura 60, collana diretta da Bruno Zevi; La Rivoluzione Informatica, sezione a cura di Antonino Saggio).
© 1999 Testo & Immagine, Turin

© 2000 Birkhäuser – Publishers for Architecture, P.O. Box 133, CH-4010 Basel, Switzerland.
Printed on acid-free paper produced from chlorine-free pulp. TCF ∞
Printed in Italy
ISBN 3-7643-6174-3
ISBN 0-8176-6174-3

9 8 7 6 5 4 3 2 1

Contents

To Denise
M.G.

To my mother, Helga
C.M.

This book originated from a series of courses entitled "The architecture of Giuseppe Terragni. Formal analysis with CAAD" given between 1991 and 1993 at the Federal Polytechnic of Zurich by Antonino Saggio. Mirko Galli's work continued as part of his degree thesis, "A critical architectural investigation using CAAD on four unbuilt projects of Giuseppe Terragni", which was presented in September 1994 and supervised by Antonino Saggio and Gerhard Schmitt. Some studies on the commemorative projects were carried out directly on the materials preserved at the Terragni Foundation Archive in Como and the authors thank the archive personnel for their willingness to help. Likewise, the renderings and analytical images in Chapter 3 were realised using a series of models created during the aforesaid course. Claudia Mühlhoff, who wrote Chapter 3, made the three-dimensional model of the Horticulturist's House, 1937 version, the three-dimensional model for the four houses by Giuseppe Terragni and the three-dimensional model of the Villa on the Lake.

The authors also thank Paolo della Casa, who made the model of the house at the Triennial, and Markus Futterknecht, who made the model of the Horticulturist's House in the 1935 version.

In addition to writing the first two chapters, Mirko Galli also coordinated the entire volume, translated part of the third chapter from German (together with Michèle Andrey), and also realised all the images and three-dimensional models in this book.

An Intelligent Model

by Antonino Saggio

To make himself understood by the workers building the dome of Santa Maria del Fiore, Brunelleschi sometimes went to the market to buy large turnips that he cut up, or also built wax or wooden models. When designing the *Opera House*, Jørn Utzon started with a sphere-orange from which he extracted the triangular segments-shells of the vaulted roof.

An extraordinary range of models has been and continues to be used by architects for their work. Today a new one is available: the computerized model. As has already been said, the world of computer science is a dynamic spider's web. We can regroup information nuclei and structure them into a myriad of relationships. We can verify the changes to an entire system made by changing an atom or, by altering the meaning, order or pattern of connections, we can form whole new worlds. In terms of power, the computerized model of a building is not just a 3D construction that offers infinite viewpoints, as does a physical model, but it is a moving model, one that is interlinked and can be changed. Its data are interrelated according to the accepted scientific definition of "model" (mathematical, financial, physical, and statistical).

Nearly all CAAD programmes now allow a hierarchical structure to be created (variously known as symbol, type, object, etc.) which represents the possibility of creating the web, the quintessence of electronic design. Let us try to understand this better. The horizontal organization into transparent layers offered by all CAAD programmes has been developed from a traditional method of working. Leaving aside the advantages of electronic data management, the process of designing by means of layers does not extend traditional possibilities, but only makes them significantly more efficient. The real innovation occurs when we turn to the vertical (and hierarchical) structure. It is now possible to organize a project using an upside-down pyramid which, through combinations of increasingly complex sets of elements, creates an extremely flexible design environment with dynamic relationships between the data. By using simulation in these environments, it is possible to examine spatial layout and construction, functional and formal organization, quantitative and economic aspects simultaneously. In this case, a CAAD project is much more than a model.

But now let us take a step backwards. What happens when we use this instrument to construct a network, a series of relationships in a building or in a project that has already been realized? This is the topic that this book aims to examine.

To start with, we reach a first, so-called easy level, which is readily understood but nonetheless decisive. Projects are often discovered, including major works, which have never been built. Seeing the *Danteum* or the Brera project, or the E42 competition by Terragni, realized during the course of the same experience at Zurich Polytechnic but not presented here, gives us a chance to study, examine, appreciate and criticize them in depth. Like a traditional physical model, the computer offers infinite viewpoints, but with a few key advantages: the possibility of exploring inside, now frequently in "real time", even using virtual reality simulation systems, and the extraordinary ability to transpose shots and views onto film.

It goes without saying that this form of construction requires care, cognitive attention and intelligent interpretation in exactly the same way as the construction of a traditional model.

This exercise can often be linked to a specific and original philological analysis. Mirko Galli's study of Terragni's commemorative projects is carried out with particular care. One need only consider the history, events and different versions of the projects for Roberto Sarfatti's tomb to perceive Terragni's research. I believe that this contribution, which differs diametrically from others on the same subject, will become a point of reference.

But while in all this the computer offers an eminently practical advantage (it is now easy to convert the electronic model back into a traditional model created using automatic cutting machines linked to the computer), the essential transition allowed by electronics is, as always, linked to the theme of dynamic interconnections.

A computerized model is a sort of intelligent model because it captures, condenses and organizes information according to the cognitive and organizational structure of whoever builds it. The long hours taken to create it represent an important period of immersion: the lines and meaning of the project gradually take shape, the interrelations, the reasons, the structures become clear, hypotheses are thrown up in a constant interrogation between those involved: between the architect who designs the project and whoever is studying or reconstructing it.

All the models, images and texts in this book, even if simply descriptive at first sight, form part of this continuous interrogation. The key instrument for a dynamic and flexible model, and not just one that visualizes, is represented by the technical instrument of *Hierarchical Structures*, but the categories to be examined are eminently formative (practicability, relations with the ground, the role of additional elements or the structure), in an attempt to find the most efficient means of understanding Terragni's projects. This enables a multi-layer and multi-meaning interpretation of the models, opening up important analyses both within each particular work and extended in parallel to a series of works, as Claudia Mühlhoff does when she analyzes four of Terragni's houses simultaneously.

To sum up, these works present at least four levels that are worth emphasizing:

1. A knowledge of works that are otherwise relatively unknown. These researchers have built architectural works that had often been left at the sketch stage, and they have produced highly reliable images.

2. An in-depth study, in Galli's case, of the historiographical context of each project, carried out using first-hand research. This investigation has thrown new light on events that were previously unknown or had been poorly researched.

3. An operation of analytical disassembly and reassembly using significant categories in the design applied "horizontally" to the same project and "vertically" in the comparison of several projects.

4. A development of CAAD technologies in the hierarchical organization of models. This has allowed simulation (including real-time exploration inside the work) and critical investigation to be incorporated in a single product. Moreover, it has allowed the model to be subsequently transposed from the PC to increasingly powerful machines for real-time simulation.

The field of simulation will be considerably enlarged by this work, not only because it enables the reconstruction of a reality or idea that has been lost, but which might be important or fertile, but it also provides a vast field of intellectual and compositive exploration. The meaning of the word "model" is revolutionized. It is no longer a perfect and static example to be copied, but a series of carefully predetermined relationships to be explored and understood anew.

Saggio@axrma.uniroma.it

The Meaning of Historical Research

Why "Virtual Terragni"? These two words would appear to have little or nothing in common. In order to clarify their association and the research that follows, a study of both architecture and computer science, it is necessary to make a few preliminary remarks about the personality of the architect to whom this book is dedicated.

Giuseppe Terragni (Meda 1904 – Como 1943) needs no introduction. His architectural work and thought form the pivot around which the Modern Movement grew up in Italy. There has been growing interest in his work, especially over the past twenty years. He is regarded by many as the most important figure of Italian rationalism, as well as undoubtedly the most original and innovative. In the past few years, new studies, a conference and a major retrospective exhibition have contributed to a fuller understanding of the architect from Como, raising new critical questions regarding his thought and works. One need only cite the Casa del Fascio in Como, designed and built between 1932 and 1936, which has been the subject of countless critical interpretations, but also the *Novocomum* apartment house, also in Como, Villa Bianca in Seveso or the series of residential buildings in Milan (including Casa Rustici, along Corso Sempione, designed with Pietro Lingeri).

Terragni was a prolific designer. Over ninety projects can be directly attributed to him during his short but intense career (not to mention the variations for each project, which were sometimes numerous), dating from 1926 when he was still a student at Milan Polytechnic, until his death shortly after his return from the Russian front. Of these, only a small number – twenty-four, to be exact – were realized, some of which number among the masterpieces of Italian architecture.

Many extremely interesting projects, sometimes drawn in intricate detail, sometimes only roughed out in a series of sketches, were never realized; but the drawings and sketches are still preserved, above all in the archives of the Terragni Foundation in Como. Some have been published in the first monographs dedicated to Terragni, like the special issue of *L'Architettura – cronache e storia* published in July 1968.

The analysis of these drawings and sketches is a fascinating field of research, flanking the study of works that were built in an attempt to make a correct evaluation of the architect's work, his composition methods, cultural references and sources of inspiration. It also helps us to understand the design process, from the conception of an idea to its definition on paper and the different variations. This book describes the study of two series of unbuilt works, now destroyed or totally modified and therefore no longer real (namely, which are no longer present or have never existed in reality). These projects are dedicated to two key themes in Terragni's architecture and the historical period in which he worked: the private house and the commemorative building. These themes accompanied Terragni throughout his creative life.

The study of an unbuilt project often involves coming into contact with approximate material, consisting of sketches and drawings whose interpretation is often complex and contradictory given that there is no finished work to act as a reference. This makes it particularly laborious to understand and analyze a project. This study was carried out by applying concepts belonging to information technology to architecture, and using the computer as a critical instrument. The computer and its laws served as the pivot around which the study was conceived and developed, applying concepts that are only apparently extraneous to architecture, but which in practice are fundamental for every researcher.

"Virtual Terragni" is therefore also the contrary: Terragni made real, tangible, discernible, an architect who can be approached with new enthusiasm and curiosity.

1. The Role of the Computer

1.1 A Growing Presence

Over the past fifteen years we have witnessed an enormous development in computer technology. Computers are now part of every cultural and administrative institution, one sits on every researcher's desk, and it would be anachronistic to write even a simple text using a normal typewriter. Not least, this extraordinary spread of the computer through business and everyday life is also directly linked to the development of interfaces based on intuitive use, and the widespread use of the mouse as an instrument for communicating with the computer. The availability of powerful models that are relatively small and attractively priced, together with the spread of extremely efficient and user-friendly software, has done the rest, even in architecture. In the field of architectural training, numerous courses are now available alongside traditional courses in which the computer and its possible applications play a central role.

Until now, historical research and architectural criticism have only occasionally used the possibilities offered by these techniques and the related organizational concepts. Moreover, computers have often been used in a way that is totally secondary to the aims of the research, being limited to the creation of databases (namely lists of data with varying levels of complexity) or the presentation and diffusion of results (notably through the spread of multimedia CD). In this study of two series of unbuilt projects by Giuseppe Terragni, the computer and the organizational concepts typical of information science play a key role, and the study was conceived and has been developed around them. Here the computer is not merely used as a means of producing images or storing data, but it acts as the researcher's privileged partner, supporting the process of analyzing, interpreting, understanding and illustrating the projects studied. In order to understand how this is possible, we should dwell for a moment on some of the basic characteristics of computerized data management and illustrate how they can be adapted to the study of architecture.

1.2 Structuring Data

The study of a work of architecture always follows a conscious or unconscious process of analysis. The accomplishment of this process is a complex intellectual operation: the simple application of a method to the initial situation is not enough to guarantee that a result will be achieved. The researcher, his intuition, his personality, the constant confrontation with the methodological process, the initial hypotheses and the results achieved, all play a central role and form a vital part of this process. The researcher comes into contact with a vast amount of information that must be given a structure, and he too produces information: hypotheses, intermediate results and conclusions, all of which must be communicated and organized for subsequent use.

Computer technology offers an easy method for managing large quantities of data, which can be modified infinitely. However, the most important possibility offered is that of defining relationships between the data, structuring them, making them interdependent, in a way that is convenient for their intended use. For example, if we modify the computer representation of a window set in a wall – by lengthening it, for instance – all the related data, if structured accordingly, will be automatically modified, as will the quantity of light penetrating the room, the perimeter of the joints, and so on.

Architectural research too uses data structures in which the data may come in any number of forms: the history of the project, its components, and archive materials are just a few examples. This information is gradually interconnected by the researcher, usually at a purely mental level (with the enormous drawback that the data cannot preserve these relationships if another researcher works on them). This is why it would be interesting to apply the systems of data interconnection used by information technology to the study of architecture.

The structure of data is sometimes defined by the software application because the person who has developed the package has ensured that the data input will be structured in a particular way that is consistent with the possible operations to be performed by the user. At other times, the structure must be painstakingly built up, because the operations available are not suited to the type of data input, or do not allow the required interconnections. The purpose of interconnecting data is to allow simulations.

1.3 Simulation and the Model

Simulation is a fundamental process in architecture and it is achieved using the *model*. Constructing a model is a method of simulation: as certain data are changed, the model shows the repercussion of changes on the entire system, consistent with the links between the data, namely the *structure*. 3D models, drawings, but also calculations or project lists, thermal or static tests are all commonly used models that simulate the various aspects of the construction to which they refer.

By exploiting the advantages of data structure offered by the computer, a computer model built to analyze a work of architecture will not only provide a 3D representation of the work, but it will also allow simulations to be performed, changing the data or the relations between them as we would do in any other model using economic, climate or social data. If the structure of the data is suitable for the simulation, we can then check hypotheses, propose scenarios and variations, acting on the parameters defined in the model.

The construction of a computerised 3D model is a rigorous process. The computer does not allow approximation. The construction process itself provides an opportunity to acquire an in-depth knowledge of the project studied. This is all the more important for a computerized model as it compels the user to obtain a precise understanding of the geometric characteristics of each element in order to create it.

The use of *solid modeling* to realise the model usually provides a choice of methods for the construction of every desired 3D component; it is left to the researcher to choose the method that leads, through a series of operations, to the realization of complex geometric components. The result of this process is a 3D model of the project being studied, obtained by simply assembling the parts, like an architectural model-maker would do. Often the software application used provides a series of basic geometric solids that can be used to build more complex 3D structures using simple assembly or *Boolean operations*: the new solid is defined as the intersection or union of the other two solids, or as the product of subtracting the volume of one solid from the other. For example, in this way it is possible to obtain a "doughnut" by subtracting a cylinder from a sphere. Solids can be also be created from 2D forms using *extrusion operations* (the 3D element is generated by sliding a flat figure consisting of any number of sides – an open or closed polygon – along a spatial vector) or *rotation operations* (the 3D element is generated by rotating an open or closed polygon around an axis).

The model is usually characterized by a level of *abstraction*, which is set at the start of the modeling process. The operator modeling the various 3D parts decides what detail to use when modelling a particular component. This enables him to exclude from the model parts that are not required by the planned simulation, thus restricting the level of detail needed. Once the model has been assembled, it is possible to alter data or modify their relationships using *tools* that, by changing the previously set parameters (e.g. position, size, colour, etc.), display the results and therefore enable the simulation.

Models constructed using this procedure consist of a series of 3D components simply combined. Relations between the (basically geometric) project data are therefore purely positional: the model simulates the reciprocal position that the elements would occupy in reality (even if freed from construction constraints and related to the initial level of abstraction). The level of simulation allowed is therefore predominantly 3D: we can visualize the project being studied, we can understand its spatial organization, check the effects of light (if the application allows us to set these parameters), check the spatial transparency, for example, or explore it by moving the elements (namely, changing the relationships between them). However, were we to decide that all vertical load-bearing elements must be red when building the model, and the non-load-bearing ones transparent (in order to highlight the flexibility of the structure), we would also establish a conceptual relationship (within the model, through the presence of two colours), as well as exploring the spatial relationships between load-bearing and non-load-bearing elements.

This relationship can be visualized using a model constructed by means of the simple spatial combination of components, but we cannot execute any simulation that involves it. This is why each load-bearing element remains individual and separate, nothing except its colour links it to the group of other elements. For example, it would not be possible to select and move all the load-bearing elements in the project simultaneously, unless one of the software tools enabled us to select only those of a particular colour. Therefore, in this case the data are organised using a *flat structure* (technically known as a Flat File – a simple list, without any interconnections or internal structure). However, structural patterns do exist that can establish complex relationships between data, identical to those established by the researcher between the different parts of a project during analysis, by identifying and grouping together certain elements (even if they are very different from one another) by function, material and *compositive meaning*. A model constructed in this way will not only provide a 3D representation of the work, but the structure of relationships between the data will contain a critical knowledge of the role, meaning and function of its elements.

1.4 Hierarchical Structures

One type of organization capable of giving the model a structure that suits the mental process of architectural analysis is *hierarchical structuring*. In a hierarchical structure, the data are organized in a sequential pattern, moving through successive groups. Data are divided into sets and the data in a set are linked to the data in another set by a hierarchical concept: this means (in organizational terms) that elements in the second set can be co-ordinated (or related) with *a single element* in the first set. One way of imagining this is to visualize the hierarchical structure as a father-son relationship between data. A son (an element in the second set) can only have one father (an element in the first set), whereas a father can have many sons. Naturally, there are no sons without fathers, except at the top of the structure. This hierarchy, which is reminiscent of a family tree, can be implemented perfectly when analyzing a work of architecture. Let us see how.

Every 3D part of the model is modeled in turn, starting with a series of *primitive* or simple geometric solids, realized by the user depending on the methods described above. Instead of constructing all the parts and then combining them one by one to make the finished model, some of the *primitive* solids are inserted (having modified their size and position, namely, their parameters) with others and then saved (using a different name) in a new entity, known as the *object*. The primitive form is not part of this object, but only its *reference*, or derivative, a symbol of the primitive form to which it is co-ordinated. The computer simply remembers that the object contains a series of references to given primitive solids, and it memorizes the changes (parameters) made by the user. In order to display a reference, the computer reads the data defined by the corresponding primitive form and applies the parameters. A father-son relationship is therefore created between the primitive form and the reference, resulting in considerable savings in terms of memory usage and, hence, increased power of display. This process can be developed in a sequential manner. Each object can be used (namely, referred anew, together with objects) as a partial component of another object at a higher level (the load-bearing walls object and pilaster object can be referred to the load-bearing elements object, an object from another class). The object is a partial component of the project: part of the transparent surfaces of the building, part of the load-bearing elements (all the walls, but not the pilasters), all the spaces with double height ceilings (in other words, in negative), etc. In order to model a pilaster, we take the primitive cube and, having altered its dimensions, we insert it into an object called 40x40 pilaster, which in turn can be referred a number of times to an object called ground floor pilasters. And so on. The system is called *hierarchical structuring* because the model is assembled using a series of objects which, in turn, are assembled from simpler objects, produced by assembling a number of simple primitive geometric shapes. A series of objects modeled on the same rung of the hierarchical ladder constitutes a class.

By defining a modeling strategy (namely, deciding what objects will be constructed, starting with what and at what point in the process), the researcher determines the final structure of the model. By subdividing the elements into objects and the objects into classes, he carries out an analytical process, with the result that the structure he builds contains a critical knowledge of the project, and some hypotheses regarding the meaning of its compositive elements. At the end of this process we will have a model that looks identical to any other digital model, but which is in fact completely different. The model now has a structure that is consistent with the critical analysis of the project, and can also simulate the compositive properties of its components, as well as every 3D characteristic. The use of hierarchical structures therefore imposes the need to reflect before starting on the type of structure to be given to the data in the model. You have to know how to proceed, decide which elements are to be built first, which primitive solids are to be used, how many hierarchical levels are required. In this sense, the process is dual: *analysis and reconstruction are complementary and also co-penetrating*. The end result is a model that contains both.

As Saggio has emphasized on several occasions in his articles on the subject, the organization of data is both constructive (from the bottom of the hierarchy to the top, necessary to the construction of the model) and semantic (from top to bottom, the result of the project's interpretation). The computer becomes the partner in this critical analysis, which flanks the realization of the model. Hierarchical structuring has the following characteristics:

- The objects are assembled in a different setting compared to the end model; this means that the work is precise and not disturbed by the presence of useless elements. The complete model will emerge at the end of the process from the assembly of the objects at the top of the hierarchy;

- The objects in the model can be visible or hidden, they can be repositioned, but only as sets of elements (in the finished model it is not possible to move or cancel an element forming part of an object: once referred, these are indissolubly linked together; an element can only be canceled by editing the object that contains it and canceling it or making it invisible).

We can edit an object to make changes to its parameters (change dimensions, position, colour, etc.), but only with reference to the component groups;
- An essential property of the structure is that any alteration to a reference or primitive element (change of colour, position, added element) affects all the references in higher classes, up to the finished model.
These properties allow an optimal simulation of the hypothetical materialization. Characteristics like material, transparency and reflection are set at the first level of the model, (through the creation of a series of primitive forms that differ for each of the materials present), but at a higher level each element made from this material will retain the reference to its own primitive form and therefore to the material characteristics defined by it. As a result, just by modifying one material parameter at the lowest hierarchical level of the model, it will be possible to repeat the modification through all of its references. This means it is easy to display different hypotheses regarding the presence of different materials in the model. If no hierarchical structure were used, the alternative would be to alter these characteristics one by one through the whole model, element by element, thus making it practically impossible to perform any simulation. A useful feature for teaching and architectural criticism is that the model can be taken apart following its own semantic structure. This means that formal or functional structural relations within the project can be explained and understood using special methods of display. The interactivity of a model based on hierarchical structures and its unlimited ability to be manipulated enable it to be used as a real working tool for verifying hypotheses and proposing new theories of interpretation. All using a simple personal computer. Data can now be organized using software designed for personal computers, not just by programmes used by large research centres. The models that can be realized are smaller (in computer terms), and can therefore be constructed and used with less powerful computers. The reduced dimensions can be explained by the structure of the data: the computer does not memorize all the model's elements, but only the

primitive solids and their parameters and the position of the objects. From an analytical point of view, a hierarchically structured model embodies a series of knowledge and the interpretations that have led to its construction. In operational terms, on the other hand, it allows every type of alternative simulation at a constructional, architectural, formal or functional level. Spatial simulation, critical analysis, the ability to modify the project elements, the simulation of alternative hypotheses and displays, are combined to form a single product. Used in this way, the computer fulfils two specific tasks: one is to become a rigorous mental instrument for critical analysis, whose use implies the need to complete the mental processes that are central to the analytical process, and the other is as a privileged means of communication and visualization.

2. Commemorative Projects

2.1 Materials

The commemorative projects represent an important group of Terragni's projects that have been analyzed through the realization of computer models based on hierarchical structuring. Between 1925 and 1943 Terragni designed twelve buildings or compositions linked to the theme of commemoration or sacredness, whether related to faith or the commemoration of the dead, to heroes or man's great achievements. Of these twelve projects, Terragni would only complete six: the War Memorial in Erba (1926–32), the Ortelli (1930), Stecchini (1931) and Pirovano (1931) tombs, the War Memorial in Como (version from a sketch by Sant'Elia, 1931–33) and the monument to Roberto Sarfatti (1932–38). The other six: the War Memorial in Como (1925 version), the cathedral in reinforced concrete (versions of 1932 and 1943), the Land Reclamation monument (1932), and the Pirovano (1928 version) and Mambretti (1936–38) tombs would remain on paper, together with the four variants of the aforesaid monument to Roberto Sarfatti.

These projects were distributed uniformly throughout Terragni's working life and they were on his drawing board at the same time as many other projects. He studied these themes in great depth, constantly jotting down new ideas, as is shown by the surviving documents, including numerous sketches (some of which are tiny) that capture an idea, a compositive solution. These projects, and in particular the tombs, form a series of small commissions to which Terragni appears to have dedicated special care and attention, preparing a number of variations for some of them. Unlike the other themes present in the architect's work, in particular his residential projects, many have claimed to see a linear pattern in the development of the commemorative theme that gradually broke away from the "Novecento" influence and became increasingly and more firmly aligned with the Modern Movement. But this is only partly true: the early projects on commemorative themes already contained the design paradigms that were to become fully developed in the years to come. This basic consideration urged us to make a more detailed analysis that would highlight Terragni's design choices and the compositive similarities between his earlier and later projects.

Terragni worked on commemorative themes both on commission and on his own initiative. He sought solutions to the commemorative theme that were compatible with the principles of modern architecture. Many cultural circles still refused to recognize the capacity of modern architecture to resolve this tricky design theme using its own principles and new materials (above all, reinforced concrete). It was widely felt that the new style could only be applied to residential architecture, factories, roads, etc., leaving churches and monuments to the classic forms of expression. In an article published in *Rassegna Italiana* by Gruppo 7, of which Terragni had been a founder member since 1926 together with Figini, Pollini, Frette, Larco, Libera, and Rava, he wrote: "[…] But everyone or nearly everyone in Italy refuses to accept that reinforced concrete can achieve monumental values. Nothing could be further from the truth: if any material can achieve classic monumentality, it is precisely reinforced concrete." Using the principles of modern architecture, the members of Gruppo 7 attempted to resolve the

PROJECT FOR THE WAR MEMORIAL IN COMO, 1926

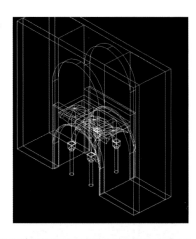

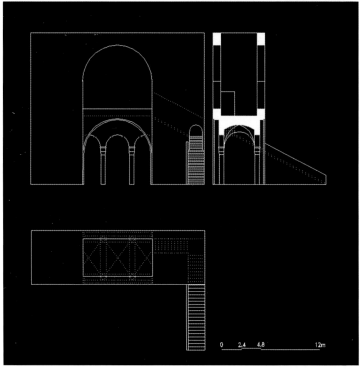

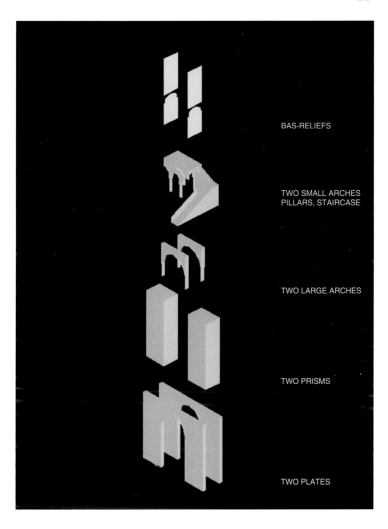

BAS-RELIEFS

TWO SMALL ARCHES
PILLARS, STAIRCASE

TWO LARGE ARCHES

TWO PRISMS

TWO PLATES

Project for the War Memorial in Como, 1926. Exploded axonometry of the project parts.

dichotomy between meaning and allegory, inevitably present in commemorative composition; in addition to the ability to be identified (in classical architecture this is the task of composition), this presupposed a rhetorical and allegorical force (previously delegated to ornamentation). Tomb and monument are the two symbolic themes of this confrontation. The primacy of form, repeatedly asserted as the basis for the new aesthetics in the articles written by Gruppo 7, made it impossible to delegate meaning and allegory to two separate components. They would inevitably coincide in form or, better, as Argan argued, "in a functionality that is neither technical nor utilitarian, and is therefore intrinsic to form and sublimated through it". Right from the outset this approach led to a process of simplification, the gradual reduction of elements, and the contraction and refinement of Terragni's ideal program to small objects (tombs) or large monuments whose composition was fully determined by a few key elements.

Rather than an evolution, Terragni's approach to the theme of commemoration can be seen as a decisive rupture, evident from his earliest works, in which the rhetorical and allegorical component blends with form, using a reduced number of elements to create a new vocabulary able to respond to the manifold and unique requirements of the theme. Often with limited distributive requirements and compositive elements, this theme provided Terragni with an opportunity to try out new typological and formal solutions that he used to perfect and enrich the modern language, giving it the authority, heretofore denied, to be an integral part of modern architectural production. A study of Terragni's commemorative buildings therefore means focusing attention on privileged creative moments that stand out owing to the overwhelming desire to experiment new solutions. It means searching for new stimuli for analysis and discovering constants that have not yet been highlighted in this great architect's work.

2.2 Strategies and the Structure of Models
Faced with the theme of commemoration and an analytical process to be carried out, not on each single project but on a

series of projects, it is important to clarify the purpose of the analysis in order to define the most suitable hierarchical structure. Starting with the most basic primitive solids, the computerized models should allow the reconstruction of the project elements, the analysis of the materials used and, most important, the attribution of a compositive meaning to the elements. The structure of the model would therefore allow the identification of those elements (or groups of elements) that fulfilled an important role in the composition, based on the four categories regarded as being of interest: *relation with context*, *mass*, *practicability* and *verticality*. These widely differing requirements (first in terms of understanding and then analysis) led to the decision to define an initial model structure, which would then be partly broken down and recomposed to form a second structure specifically conceived for the analysis. The end result was a series of models whose structure was based on hypotheses regarding the compositive role of the elements; but it also led to a series of photo-realistic images of the projects and a series of scaled drawings and axonometries showing the projects. In the absence of archive material of equal value, the latter would explain the construction hypotheses relating to the size of the various components.

In the simplest situation, each element of the model is a reference to an initial *cube*, whose parameters have been set to give the right shape and size. In order to allow this structure to simulate materials, the initial *cube* has been referenced to a series of objects in a first class, namely, the *materials*: one object for each supposed material present in the project in question. By referencing the objects in the material class, we produce the objects in the *project elements* class, so that each element can be traced back to a single material (according to the characteristic scheme used by hierarchical structuring). The elements are referenced to a higher class in other objects, the key groups of the project. These are then referenced in the end model. Exploded axonometries, technical drawings and photo-realistic views of each project were then made. The set hierarchical structure allowed the models to be broken down with ease and material qualities could be attributed to the various parts.

PROJECT FOR THE LAND
RECLAMATION MONUMENT,
1932

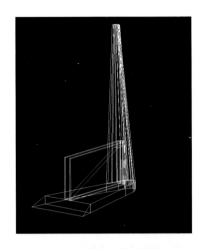

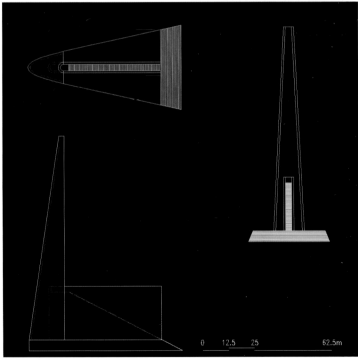

0   12.5   25   62.5m

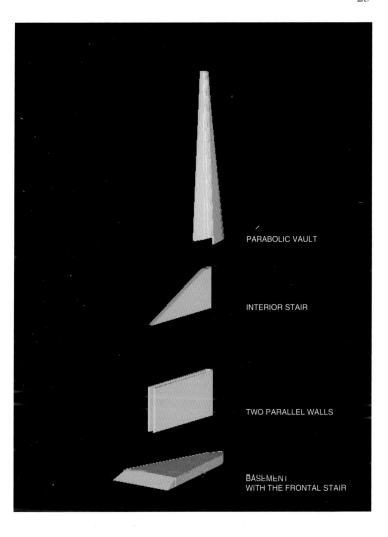

PARABOLIC VAULT

INTERIOR STAIR

TWO PARALLEL WALLS

BASEMENT
WITH THE FRONTAL STAIR

Project for the Land Reclamation Monument, 1932, exploded axonometry of the project parts.

2.3 Understanding the Projects

The wide variety of archive sources in terms of the completeness of their description, the limited number of elements in each project, as well as the complex shape of some elements made it necessary to tackle the problem of their correct 3D reproduction, trying to interpret the available sources. First of all, the projects needed to be understood, determining the shape and size of the primary elements, and their position compared to other elements or sets of elements. Moreover, it was necessary to assess the degree of detail required for their 3D representation. The first project in which Terragni explored the commemorative building theme was the project for a War

20-21 Memorial in Como. It was linked to the two-stage competition announced in Como in 1926 for the design and construction of a monument that would commemorate the death of soldiers from Como in the First World War.

The proposed site of the future construction was the heart of Como's historic centre: the area between the cathedral, the medieval town hall, the "Broletto", and the bell-tower of the Basilica of San Giacomo. The project by Terragni and Lingeri passed through to the second round and was classified in second place, in spite of changes made. Later, not even the winning project by Asnago and Vender was built because in 1928 the Town Council refused to grant permission to use the area. Terragni and Lingeri's project borrowed in part from an earlier proposal made on the same theme by Federico Frigerio in 1923. It proposed the reconstruction of the original façade of the Basilica of San Giacomo, beside the cathedral, which had been demolished and pushed further back in the 16th century. Terragni and Lingeri took up this idea as part of a different approach in which the project acquired its own autonomy and became a key new element in the urban context: a permeable diaphragm that redefined the relationship between the two squares in the centre of Como. The architects proposed an archeological comparison with these earlier buildings by erecting a wall, perforated by an arch, in front of the pronaos of the basilica. The arch resembled a triumphal arch, but in fact consisted of two thin walls, close enough together to form a body that could be traversed frontally, containing the indispensable rhetorical elements for this type of monument as bas-reliefs on the internal walls.

The second project by Terragni examined here is the Land Reclamation monument of 1932, which has a relatively con- 24-28 fused history and is very poorly documented. The archive material on this project in fact consists of two photos of the metal model of the monument, which has now been lost. The land reclamations in question were those started towards the end of the Twenties under the Fascist regime. Through the systematic use of large investments and massive human resources, they aimed to reclaim those areas of Italy that were still uncultivated because the land was swampy and unhealthy, and to redistribute the land to colonies of farmers. The project, which Terragni drew up in 1932, must be set against this epic of Mussolini's rule. Together with others, the project was sent to the Exhibition of Rationalist Architecture held in Florence in March that year, an important promotional opportunity to publicize rationalist ideas and to gain the support of public opinion. The history of Terragni's project is completely unknown and no sketches or plans of the project exist or have been identified. It is also not known why Terragni chose to celebrate these land reclamations: was it the outcome of a particular commission that was then annulled, or a promotional exercise undertaken by the architect? Given the approximate nature of all planning schemes linked to the land reclamation projects, the idea of a personal exercise to mark the occasion of an architectural exhibition appears to be the most probable.

The project consists of four elements, two of which are extremely complex. The first element is the basement, which is wider at the front and rounded at the back. A broad flight of steps rests on the basement, bringing the visitor up to this first level. Starting from the rounded extremity, a vertical parabolic arch stands on the basement, 100 metres high and tapering at the top. Two 20-metre-high walls, only five metres apart and containing a narrow flight of stairs, complete the composition. The monolithic nature of the monument and the complexity and size of its parts, as well as the fact that it cele-

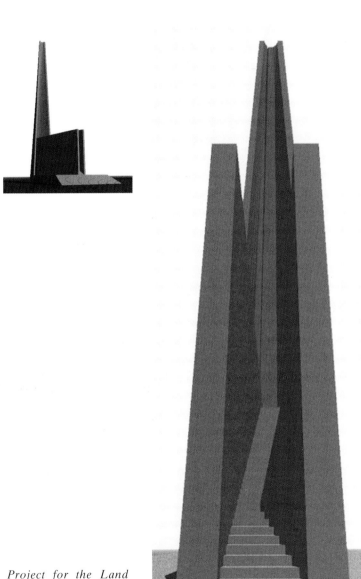

Project for the Land Reclamation Monument, 1932, rendering.

PROJECT FOR THE CATHEDRAL IN
REINFORCED CONCRETE, 1932,
RENDERING

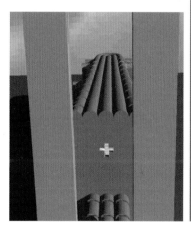

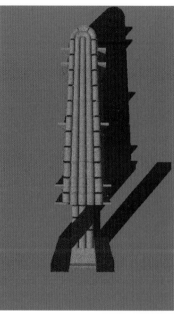

brated man's victory over nature are characteristics that point to concrete as the only material that could be used for its construction. In this, as well as in its dimensions and the complexity of its forms, it resembles the contemporary project for a cathedral in reinforced concrete.

Each project has been reproduced using a 2D image (fronts, plan and section, obtained using the views from the 3D model), an overall 3D view of the project (axonometry) and an exploded axonometry obtained by spacing out the objects in the finished model. Exploding the model was a very simple operation given that the elements in each group could not be moved separately, but only together. The top hierarchical level in fact only included groups of elements forming objects that were considered relevant to an explanation of the project in compositive terms. Alongside the undoubted practicality (outside elements do not complicate the vision and comprehension of the object, which can be carefully positioned at a higher hierarchical level), hierarchical structuring also offers the advantage of visualizing all the components of the model together, but separately (in individual modeling windows), simplifying their complexity and the relations established by the researcher between the components. Moreover, the possibility of dynamically changing point of view allows the best view of the model to be shown each time.

The fact of not being free to intervene on each part of the finished model might appear a limitation. But this particular feature fully illustrates the potential of hierarchical structuring and highlights the role of control over the process of analytical interpretation that proceeds alongside the process of 3D reconstruction. As was pointed out earlier, in order to simulate the different semantic properties of an element in a set (namely the fact that it belongs to one group rather than another), the researcher must also rethink the position of the element inside the hierarchical structure.

2.4 Hypotheses of Reality

Having understood the projects in terms of forms and the geometric relations between the elements, the next step was to hypothesize their material characteristics, and to study the effect of the volumes and surfaces under the light.

The project for a cathedral in reinforced concrete again dates 29 from 1932. It was also conceived for the exhibition in Florence, together with the Land Reclamation monument. The project should be seen as a purely stylistic exercise, a compositive manifesto of Terragni's ideas on the commemorative theme. Terragni prepared extremely detailed drawings for this project, in particular for the structure of the cathedral shell, which were preceded by a long series of sketches. Terragni returned to the cathedral theme just before his death in a series of sketches that are not easy to interpret, as if searching for other possible solutions to the theme. The 1932 project is the only one that was studied in detail, together with the monumental project on a larger scale conceived by Terragni.

Like the design for the Land Reclamation monument, the Cathedral in reinforced concrete is made up of a small number of extremely complex elements, blended together without breaks. The liturgical space is housed within a single shell, 30 metres wide and 35 metres high: this is the most complex part of the project. Four gigantic frames support a roof consisting of a series of five cone-shaped half-vaults, tapering towards the apse, where the structure turns over to form the apsidal zone. A wall hangs down from outside the half-vaults, like a curtain. It contains a series of high, narrow slits that echo the rhythm of the roof and run from the roof down to 9 metres above floor level.

A fifth frame forms the front of the church and closes the space in the entrance area. Depending on the various models, this is either covered by a portico or uncovered, and Terragni shifts the entry level into the church either in front or behind the two bell towers, depending whether the stair leading up to the church is in front or between them. Built entirely in reinforced concrete, the cathedral has a simple interior that is nonetheless extremely effective, enabling the light to highlight the complex shape of the roof.

The projects for the Mambretti tomb, designed by Terragni 32-33 for the cemetery in Fino Mornasco between 1936 and 1938,

PROJECT FOR THE MAMBRETTI TOMB, 1936–38

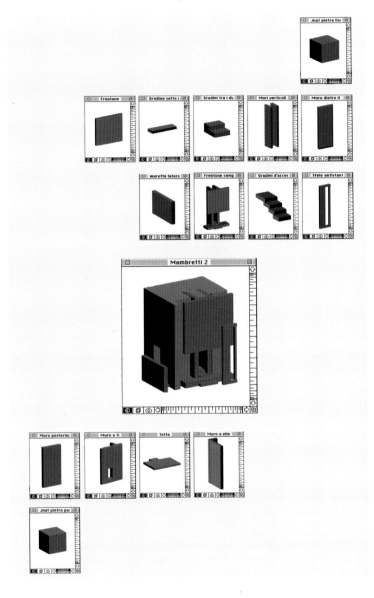

Facing page: the 3D model of the square plan version, broken down according to its own hierarchical structure. This page, top: the square plan version; bottom: the model with a rectangular plan.

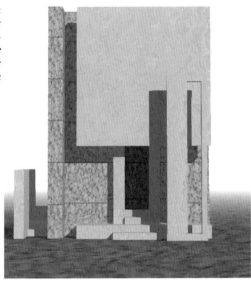

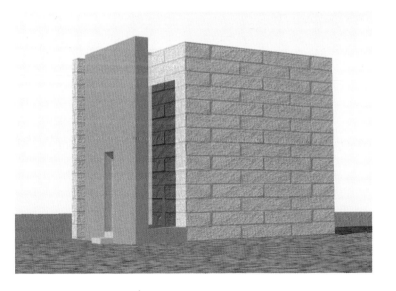

were never realized. Terragni designed two versions containing all his main architectural themes, almost an ultimate refinement of his approach to the monumental theme. The tomb stands in a corner of the cemetery, and the projects highlight the singular layout of the two entrances, thus making it possible to enter outside normal hours.

Terragni devised a solution with a square plan, in which two thin slabs on the façade identified the entrance and supported a large square stone slab and a rectangular one. The entrance is a hole in the main façade, the narrow one facing the cemetery, which in composition terms is separated from the prism but at the same time helps to define it. The dual entrance enhances both compositions by creating a spiral path from the outside into the center and then down into the basement, a path which is also identified in the second variant by the walls folding towards the inside of the prism. A few well-matched elements and the dynamic nature of all Terragni's commemorative works combine here to give identity and allegory.

The hierarchical structure of the models is particularly useful in this case and was also designed to check a number of hypotheses relating to the materials used by Terragni in his projects. These hypotheses were introduced into the structure at the level just above the primitive forms. Each component of the project is a reference not to a single geometric primitive shape, but rather to a series of different primitive forms, each of which is associated with a material present at the lowest hierarchical level of the projects, from which the various geometric shapes are then referenced. It is worth noting that the inclusion of material characteristics at a primitive level of the hierarchical structure enables materialization hypotheses to be simulated, but does not impose restrictions on the main field of inquiry, namely, compositive analysis.

In order to study the different materials, it is necessary to use a rendering program to assign different material attributes (grain, transparency, brilliance, mapping, etc.) to each geometric component in the model. Adequate ambient lighting is also needed (also creating cast shadows and shaded objects) to display the different hypotheses regarding the real appear-

PROJECT FOR THE MONUMENT TO ROBERTO SARFATTI, 1932–35

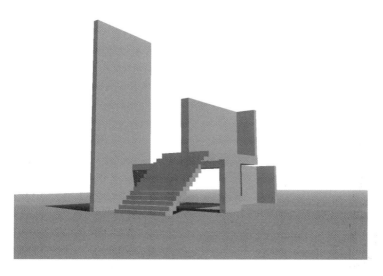

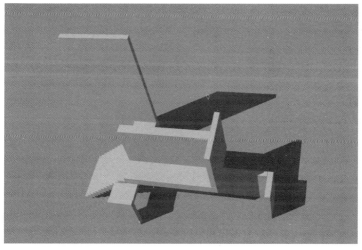

First version.

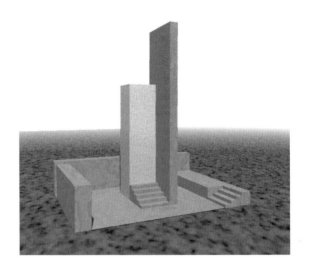

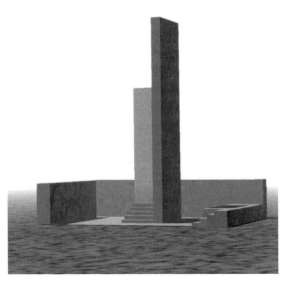

Project for the Monument to Roberto Sarfatti, second version. Facing page: third version.

ance of the project. The full implications of the hierarchical organization of data now become apparent: when assigning certain material characteristics to different geometric elements, we need only assign them to the corresponding primitive element. The program will then automatically assign the characteristics (if the hierarchical structure is correct) to all the geometric references of the primitive element at a higher hierarchical level. In a trice, using simple geometric figures in an environment unrelated to the model itself, the chosen material characteristics will have been attributed to all the elements (whether there are five, fifty, or five hundred). If the program used to realize the model does not include rendering options, the model must be exported to another program, taking care to keep the hierarchical structure, in order to assign the material attributes to the primitive elements. This operation is often difficult: many export routines do not offer the possibility of conserving the structure, and so it is necessary to define a personalized routine.

A quick glimpse at the models will help to explain these remarks. The cathedral in reinforced concrete includes a single primitive material, whereas the Mambretti tomb contains three: smooth stone, rough stone, and glass. Each part of the model is then realized, starting with the primitive element corresponding to the component material support.

This knowledge is clearly hidden inside the hierarchical structure and cannot be visualized in 3D models: however, simulation can take place because it is innate in the structure. It is impossible to explode the model using groups of elements in the same material, because this would imply the need for a different structure enabling this type of analysis, which is not the most important, although the images certainly allow the projects to be viewed in a very interesting way.

2.5 To Roberto Sarfatti, 1932–35

Are there constants in the way Terragni handles the theme of commemoration? Can we identify a starting position (perhaps "classic" or "Novecento") from which Terragni gradually departs as he grafts in the themes of modernity? Or does the architect follow another course, is he inclined towards another type of research? What interests him most? What is he indifferent to? And in what circumstances?

The monument to Roberto Sarfatti, which Terragni started to design in 1932, was one of the very few to be finally constructed and inaugurated in 1938. It has a long and complex history and Terragni in fact prepared five different designs for this monument. These have been the subject of an analysis relating to composition categories, producing a series of analytical images as well as those already obtained for the other projects. 35-61

Roberto Sarfatti was the eldest son of Margherita Sarfatti, an influential art critic and supporter of *Il Novecento*, who was very close to Mussolini for several years. Terragni enjoyed excellent relations with her and she often commented on his projects, sometimes disagreeing with them as in the case of the design for the Land Reclamation monument. Her son, Roberto, who enrolled as a volunteer in the "Alpini" regiment during the First World War, died heroically on 21 January 1918 at the age of seventeen in an engagement on the Ecchele Pass at Sasso, a few kilometres from Asiago. He was awarded a gold medal for military valour. It was natural that plans should be made for a commemorative monument at the site of his death (also because at the time there was also a special office for the commemoration of war victims). After a lengthy search, his body was eventually found in 1934 in the war cemetery in the nearby village of Stoccaredo.

For many years it was thought that Terragni only started work on the designs for the monument after 1934, but a letter to Margherita Sarfatti dated 12 March 1932, preserved in the Fondazione Terragni in Como, contains comments on an early design previously identified in a sketch published by Bruno Zevi in his book on Terragni and correctly indicated as forming part of Terragni's research on this monument. Other sketches that had previously been difficult to interpret, have also been linked to this project now that it has been backdated. The monument to Roberto Sarfatti is crucial for a study of Terragni's artistic personality. On the one hand, the design had to be small, but also concrete and with a marked

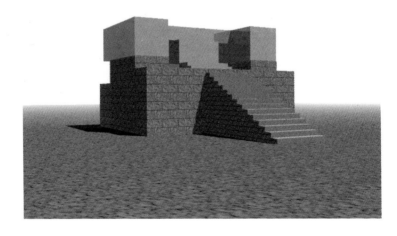

Project for the Monument to Roberto Sarfatti, fourth version. Facing page: the fifth version, which was finally built.

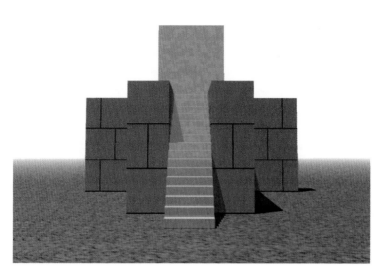

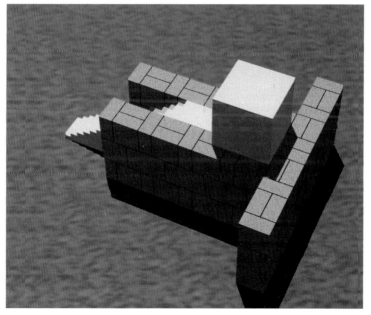

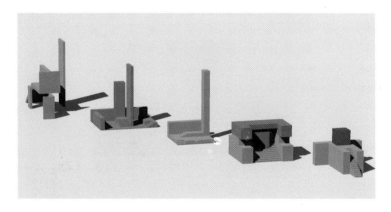

Project for the Monument to Roberto Sarfatti: the five variants for the project shown using the same scale

commemorative value that far exceeds its simple funereal function. On the other, the client was exceptionally well prepared, and therefore exacting. Terragni also dedicated considerable time and effort to the monument, re-designing it continuously for three years.

In 1932 – at the time when exhumation work had commenced, but Roberto's body had not yet been found – Terragni drew
35 up a *preliminary project*, which Margherita Sarfatti criticized as being "too playful for a tomb". It was a very free composition, unrestrained by formal rules, which used a very few elements put together in a highly original way. The project comprised an "L-shaped" element resting on its side on the ground, with the short side forming the commemorative stone and main façade of the composition. A tall, narrow stele stood a little further away, set at an angle to the main façade. A second L-shaped element was linked to the stele forming a bridge, on which rested another L-shaped element divided in two lengthways by a dividing wall, forming a level that was accessed by a broad stair. The resulting composition was very precise, but also slightly unbalanced, and was completely detached from the ground.
36 Terragni then drew up a *second project* that uses one or two

of the same elements but gives greater emphasis to the definition of the place and the axes of movement. The monument is contained in a basement at the level of the surrounding ground, and a group of elements forms a sort of enclosure measuring 6 metres by 8, closed on three sides, consisting of two walls and a low platform accessed by four steps. A tall stele stands in the centre of this enclosure, positioned at an angle, and a slightly lower monolithic block with a square base, another four steps leading up to it, acts as the commemorative stone. The composition is still extremely dynamic, but the centre of gravity is clearly determined in relation to other elements.

A *third project* simplified the affirmations made by the sec- **37** ond project, and reduced the number of elements used. The platform was raised above ground level, with three steps leading up to it and a low wall surrounding it. The stele rises up in the centre of this basement, still set at an angle compared to the direction of approach. It is reached by a further three steps. The position of the central group, which has its own sense of direction, shifts the centre of gravity, making the composition less static than the previous one, although fewer elements are used.

After this initial series of designs in 1932, Terragni returned to the problem in 1934, reviewing the layout and the component elements, perhaps on Sarfatti's suggestion and perhaps after lengthy reflections on the nature of the site chosen to build the monument: a solitary mountain pass, far from the nearest village, surrounded by the peaks of the Dolomites on the high plateau of Asiago. He drew up another two designs, which at first seem radically different and far removed from the research carried out until then. Both are documented in detailed drawings and Terragni appears to work on two parallel solutions with common characteristics. He abandoned the idea of the basement and returned to the idea of building directly on the ground; the compositions were symmetric, and from the drawings it is clear that he wished to use two different materials.

The *fourth project* is also documented through detailed work- **40** ing drawings. It consists of two side walls and one front wall, enclosing a broad staircase on one side into which the memorial stone is set, overhung by a roof, whereas on the other side of the wall Terragni included a descending staircase. In spite of the static nature and gravity of the forms and the symmetric composition, this creates a key dynamic component (crossing through), turning the monument into a live sculpture in spite of the fact that it is firmly delimited.

41 The *fifth project*, contemporary to the fourth, was finally chosen by Sarfatti and construction began. It was in fact easier to erect on such rough and inaccessible ground. It would also prove less expensive while retaining all the essential qualities. The project was based on a reduction and simplification of the elements in the fourth project and, with a little luck, it can be visited by heading towards Sasso from Asiago.

The memorial stone with the inscription ought to have been made from a single stone block, abstract and perfect, but transport difficulties made this impossible to achieve. It was carved in two parts and then assembled on the spot. All the other elements in the composition, two side walls, the front wall, and the staircase inserted between the two side walls, emerging from the composition to rest on the ground, were made from blocks of cut stone. In this symmetrical solution, the presence of the staircase is essential, as in the earlier version, although you can no longer walk through the monument.

2.6 Commemoration and Composition Categories

Four composition categories need to be analyzed and highlighted in every project: the relationship with the *context* (an understanding of the elements and the properties used by the project to relate to its own context, whether real or theoretical), *practicability* (where and how the project can be directly experienced by the user), *mass* (its size and nature, bearing in mind the unique ability of mass to evoke firmness, solidity, and hence to express presence, an important commemorative factor), and *verticality* (a category with a totemic and symbolic value). The main elements have already been identified for each project, using a process of comparison between the original materials available. They were then modeled separately,

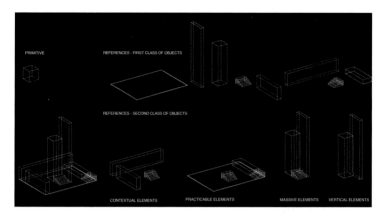

Model of the second variant for the Monument to Roberto Sarfatti broken down according to its own structure. Top: the primitive forms with their different levels of visualization. Bottom: the complete model and the four partial models that make it up.

before being assembled. In order to study the compositive meaning of the elements, this preliminary hierarchical structure had to be broken down to reach the group of *project elements*, before being re-referenced to create the objects in the group of compositive elements. These objects are the most important in the whole structure. The references for the individual project elements, all derived from the same "cubic" primitives (a cube made up of its corners alone), were re-assembled again depending on their role in the project (first, all the contextual elements, for example, followed by the practicable elements, and so on, bearing in mind that each element could form part of more than one set). At the end of this stage, four objects were obtained, consisting in turn of the most important project elements for each of the four project categories. These were then referenced to the whole model. At this point, the structure of the final model contained both a structure based on elements or sets of primary elements (referenced to the main architectural components of the project in question), and, at a higher hierarchical level, a structure based on sets (sometimes with common intersections) of these elements (and these alone). In each project the latter contributed to the manifestation of the four project categories of interest to the study.

Therefore, the 3D models contain composition information and can simulate the properties of each composition category in each project. Furthermore, if desired, they also allow the number of categories to be extended to five, without altering the structure of the model, but only by adding another object to those in the *category* class. It is important to note that, given that an element may have more than one compositive function, it may appear in more than one object in this class. This does not contradict the hierarchical principle, whereby each primitive solid (the object of the project element class) may have several references, but each reference (namely the same element within the object in the categories class) can only derive from one primitive shape. At this point it was necessary to create instruments that were better equipped for simulation and for displaying the results. We have already seen how, starting from a primitive form, hierarchical structuring enables all the other project elements to be modeled, before assembling them to form a complete model, structured by classes of objects. By altering the characteristics of the primitive forms – namely, by changing their data – it is possible to observe the repercussions of these changes at all higher levels. This property can be used to highlight one of the objects of the *categories* in relation to others inside the finished model, thereby obtaining a series of images which distinguish those elements forming part of each composition category analyzed.

These changes to primitive forms, which result in simulations, can be saved and then simply recalled, rather than being re-enacted each time by altering the attributes. In practice, changes made to the primitives alter the way they are visualized in the model. These changes are called *visualization levels*, and an indefinite number exist. A preliminary level, obtained by adding to the generic primitive (a cube made solely with lines), a level of representation in which it appears to be solid, enables the components of each set to be represented, on each occasion, as solid volumes. This occurs by choosing

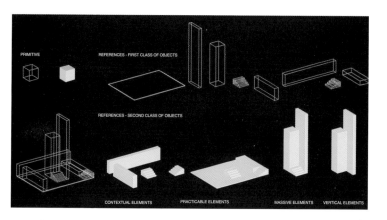

Model of the second variant for the Monument to Roberto Sarfatti broken down according to its own structure, with the addition of a visualization layer.

to represent, in the *mass elements* object, the initial cube at its second level of representation: a *solid cube*. In the final model these elements will be highlighted through comparison with others, which are still visible but only represented by the corners. This operation is only possible thanks to the special structure of the models, as the outcome of a full analysis.

It is worth noting that, in the finished model, it was no longer possible to alter the characteristics (for example, in the first solution for the monument to Roberto Sarfatti) of the entrance stairway, given that it now formed an object together with the L-shaped element at the other end of the monument: the two elements with the greatest contextual value. In the fourth version of the monument to Roberto Sarfatti, it is worth noting that at least three hierarchical levels were used for the critical analysis: the finished model, the four objects from the categories class, a series of objects at a lower hierarchical level (the single components in each group) and the primitive forms, in this case at least two different ones. In fact, the hypothesis that Terragni used two distinct materials for the various components of the project was inserted in the constructed model, in order to proceed with rendering. The single components were then modeled on the basis of two primitive forms with different colours, a characteristic that is preserved throughout the upper hierarchical levels. This series of models, each consisting of four subsets of elements, which are at first indistinguishable but can be identified simply by changing the visualization level, were then used to refine the analysis of projects.

2.7 Cross-Comparisons

Having analyzed the projects individually, a new series of images had to be created to highlight the specific properties of the elements in each project that had been previously correlated to different composition categories. The purpose was to compare the various solutions put forward by Terragni for the theme of commemorative buildings. In the previous series of images, it was sufficient to add a level of visualization to the cube-shaped primitive form, and then refer back to it for each of the four objects in the categories class (thus visualizing the solid components). The number of visualization levels was then increased as required to create comparative images:

- for the context, it was necessary to highlight the direction of the relationships and the sides of the elements supporting them;

- for practicability, the surface was required that could effectively be crossed, differentiating it into primary and secondary;

- for mass, it was necessary to indicate the ratio between virtual mass (namely, simulated mass, indicated by a grid) and real mass;

- for verticality, it was interesting to show the largest component, marking the narrowest sides of the vertical elements (or all four sides, if it was square).

This made it necessary to add ten further levels of visualization to the primitive cube. The series of images was then obtained by editing an object from the finished model, and then recalling the desired level of visualization for each component of the object.

The position of the element and its orientation in the finished model must be correct, underlining yet again the interlocutory function of the computer. In fact, if the upper side of an

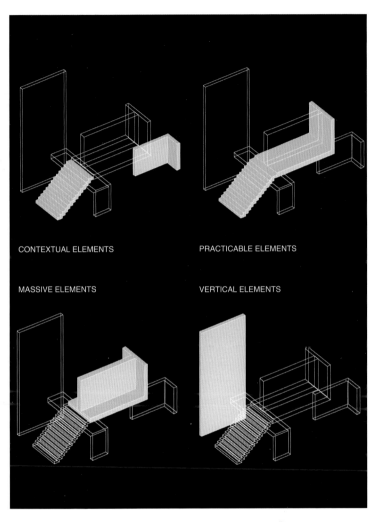

CONTEXTUAL ELEMENTS

PRACTICABLE ELEMENTS

MASSIVE ELEMENTS

VERTICAL ELEMENTS

Project for the Monument to Roberto Sarfatti, 1932–38: the compositive elements with a contextual value.

element needed to be highlighted, it was necessary to choose the level of visualization in which the upper side of the corresponding primitive shape was highlighted. This may result in

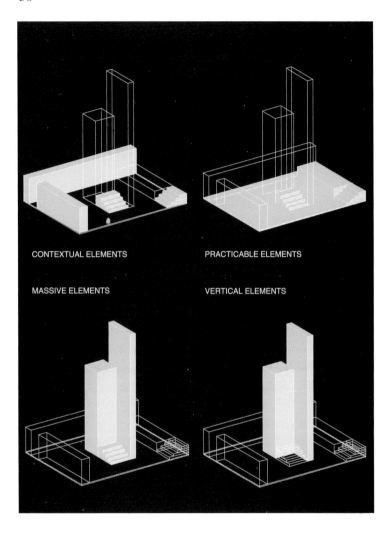

Project for the Monument to Roberto Sarfatti, 1932–38: the four categories in the second version of the project.

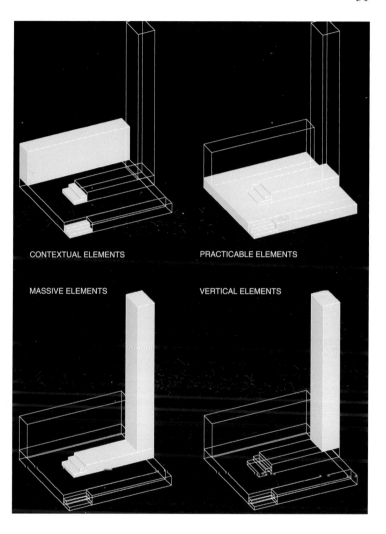

Project for the Monument to Roberto Sarfatti, 1932–38: the four categories in the third version of the project.

52

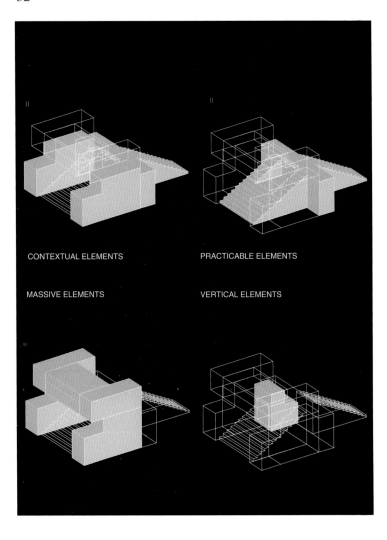

CONTEXTUAL ELEMENTS

PRACTICABLE ELEMENTS

MASSIVE ELEMENTS

VERTICAL ELEMENTS

Project for the Monument to Roberto Sarfatti, 1932–38: the four categories in the fourth version of the project.

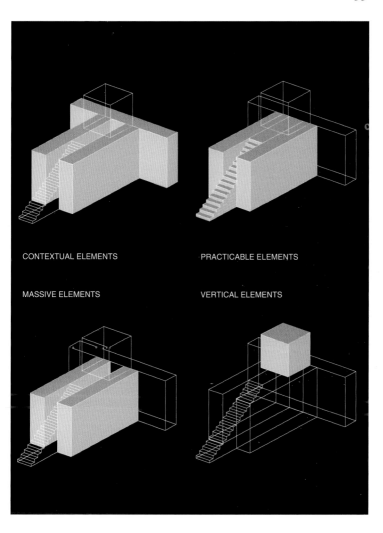

CONTEXTUAL ELEMENTS

PRACTICABLE ELEMENTS

MASSIVE ELEMENTS

VERTICAL ELEMENTS

Project for the Monument to Roberto Sarfatti, 1932–38: the four categories in the fifth version of the project

the lower side of the element being highlighted in the model, indicating that the primitive shape was referenced "upside-down". It must then be rotated to obtain the correct image.

An extra element was added to the group in the case of the mass category: the cube showing virtual mass. To do this, another parallelepiped was added to the object (after having edited it), referenced back to the *cubic* primitive. This was then visualized with red corners by creating a corresponding level of visualization for the primitive shape. The hierarchical structure of the models therefore allowed the creation of the last series of images, which sums up the entire analytical process. At the same time, the models can represent a multi-tude of starting points for further refinement of the analysis, or its extension to other composition categories.

A comparison between the images, which were subsequently mounted on boards, revealed a series of final considerations regarding the way in which Terragni approaches the com-memorative theme. Only in two solutions, namely, the War Memorial in Como and the fourth version of the Roberto Sarfatti Monument, does Terragni define an ambivalent con-textual relationship: a so-called direction of arrival, the approach, and a direction for leaving the composition. Only in these two cases does the concept of "crossing through" form part of the concept of understanding the rhetorical meaning of the object, which becomes a threshold and a pause in the path leading through it. All the other monuments represent points of arrival, at which to be captured and become part of the composition. The possibility of turning in a direction other than that used for the approach is only sometimes available, once inside the monument. This dynam-ic component is underlined by the position of the other com-positive elements.

One example of this is the early solutions for the Sarfatti monument, where the raised context, resembling an outlook point, probably made this solution logical. This secondary direction is always closely correlated with the main direction, and it emphasizes its centrality or eccentricity accordingly.

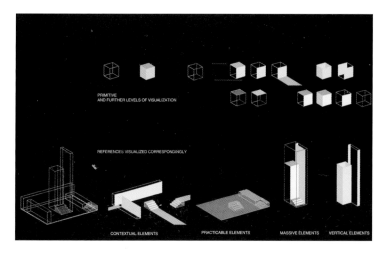

PRIMITIVE
AND FURTHER LEVELS OF VISUALIZATION

REFERENCES VISUALIZED CORRESPONDINGLY

CONTEXTUAL ELEMENTS   PRACTICABLE ELEMENTS   MASSIVE ELEMENTS   VERTICAL ELEMENTS

The model of the second variation for the monument to Roberto Sarfatti broken down according to its own structure, with the addition of the necessary visualization levels to compare the projects. Page 56: a comparison of the context category in the different versions. Page 57: a comparison of the practicability category in the different versions.

You always climb up Terragni's monuments and they can be crossed, sometimes in a complex manner, but always upwards. A practicable area is often developed at different levels, and the compositions have a summit, which can be reached, with varying degrees of difficulty, a place that offers a complete experience of the monument. It is not a difficult journey, like that designed by Terragni for the Danteum, but rather a journey of discovery, a stroll through the elements of the composition, which is assimilated and understood in its complexity. The centre of gravity is often the focal point, the magical place in which the symbolic forces of the composition are concentrated and expressed.

There is a striking difference between the real mass and the virtual mass, namely, the mass simulated but not really possessed by the monument. Terragni excavates the mass, he empties it or merely simulates it, enabling the monument to become practicable, often by inserting the stairs between two

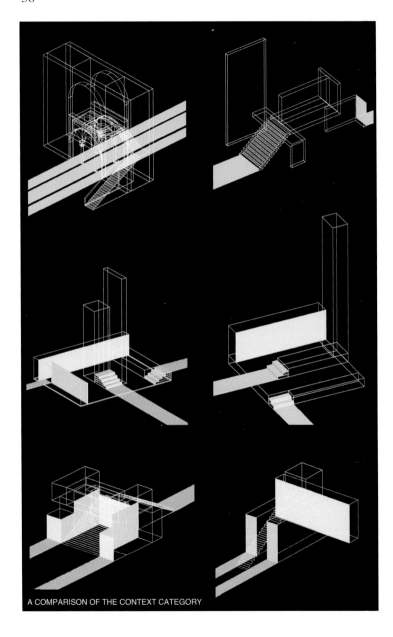

A COMPARISON OF THE CONTEXT CATEGORY

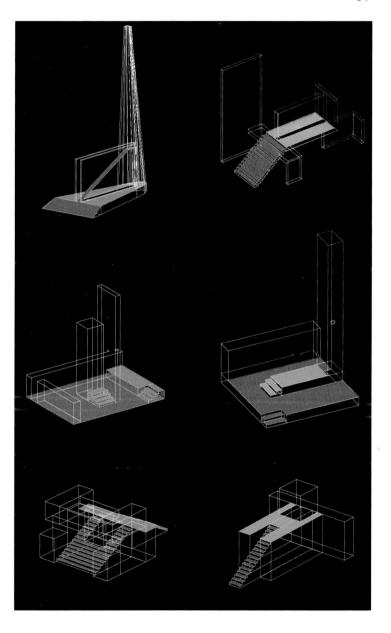

parallel walls. It always remains extremely well balanced. Terragni never shifts the centre of gravity by adopting a particular layout of the mass. Verticality has expressed the monumental nature of the work since antiquity, but in Terragni's work it is increasingly hidden inside the mass of the monument. While this is still an important component in the cathedral project, where it is conditioned by the very nature of the bell-towers, the Land Reclamation monument is an exception: its high parabolic vault remains unattainable even after the laborious climb up the long staircase.

As the context gradually becomes clearer, and this can be seen in the War Memorial and in the Sarfatti project, the vertical elements are reduced and disappear, absorbed by other elements in the composition. Terragni uses this component not only to indicate the point of arrival, but also to flank and protect it: we need only think of the steles in the Sarfatti monument, which are secondary elements in the composition, features that are external to the place of worship and only serve to support the main element. They are always seen in profile as very thin forms, indicating the direction of the monument rather than being vertical components in the classic sense of the term.

The practicability of Terragni's monuments is therefore their most significant component. From a precise and univocal relationship with the context, dictated by the type of composition (in the case of the cathedral and the Land Reclamation monument), by the existence of an urban (War Memorial) or rural (monument to Sarfatti) setting, Terragni develops a concept of practicability, moving between the definition of two levels, the ability to cross through the project and the experience of climbing up and arriving at a place. These are always easy, direct, clear, and univocal experiences. Terragni appears concerned not to leave any alternatives, to avoid distraction, to lead the visitor straight to the final destination. The rhetorical message is dynamic, it can only be understood by moving inside the composition: this is something that is true right from the earliest projects on this theme. It is an extremely modern approach that perhaps escapes first analysis.

3. Terragni's Villas: a Portfolio and an Analysis

3.1 Terragni and the Composition Theme of the House

The architectural theme of the modern house became a clear trend immediately after it first appeared in the construction of the Weissenhofsiedlung in Stuttgart in 1928, no longer being regarded as a solitary experiment for avantgarde architects.

For the rationalist architects and in particular Terragni, perhaps their most illustrious representative in Italy, the single-family house was regarded as a laboratory in which to experiment an idea and perfect it in all its artistic consequences.

This type of building, unconstrained by standards, regulations and representative aspects, offered greater freedom of design compared to other assignments, in particular in the public sector. The audacious experiments on the theme of the single-family house often seduce us with their innovative originality.

In addition to his major public projects, including the Asilo Sant'Elia (Sant'Elia Nursery School) and the Casa del Fascio in Como, Terragni devoted himself passionately to designing private houses. Of a total of eight projects, only three were actually built. All three houses have shared a common fate of disrepair, alterations, and demolition.

This has provided an even greater stimulus to this attempt to reconstruct them, enabling them to re-appear through computerized images.

3.2 Artist's Holiday House on the Lake, 1933 64-65

This project was conceived as a contribution to 5th Triennale in Milan entitled "An exhibition of modern architecture", which aimed to foster the construction of homes that were more in keeping with the spirit of the age.

Thirty experimental projects, all realized by representatives of the school of rational architecture, were constructed as pavilions in Sempione Park in Milan.

Terragni designed a holiday house on the lake for an artist and his family, together with other members of the Como

60

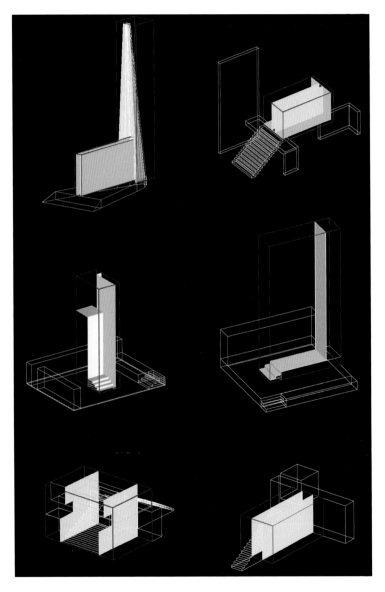

Project for the Monument to Roberto Sarfatti: a comparison of the mass category in the different versions.

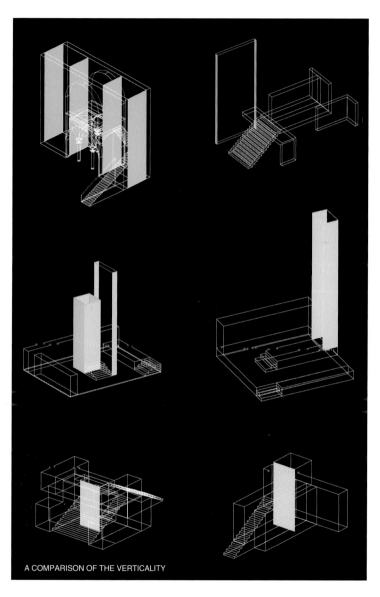

A COMPARISON OF THE VERTICALITY

Project for the Monument to Roberto Sarfatti: a comparison of the verticality category in the different versions.

Group[1]. The choice of the main layout was based on the diversity of the spaces to be linked. The three-part plan is made up of two prisms: a white prism on two levels (with daytime rooms on the ground floor and night areas on the first floor), and a second (probably red) one as the artist's workshop. Between these two cubes lay an empty space. The external space provided an original way of separating the different parts of the construction and at the same time gave them unity, creating an ambivalent play. The porch along the main façade united the external area, forming a corridor linking the two parts of the building. They therefore formed a single front façade whose tempo was enlivened by the chiaroscuro of the porch.

The rear view showed the two separate volumes whose junction, covered by the horizontal floor of terrace and its railings, ends with the workshop wall. The prism containing the residential areas is deeper than that of the workshop and encloses a rectangular paved courtyard, forming part of the L-shaped layout.

---

1. The Fifth Milan Triennale was centered on the theme of the family house, with the optimistic aim of spreading and publicizing the new materials and construction systems linked to prefabricated buildings. For a critical review of the exhibition, see the articles by E. Persico, "Gli architetti italiani", in *L'Italia Letteraria*, August 1933, and "L'architettura mondiale", in *L'Italia Letteraria*, July 1933. An analysis of the Milan Triennale can be found in the article by G. Polin, "La Triennale di Milano 1923–1947", in *Rassegna*, 1982. The Como Group consisted of the architects M. Cereghini, A. Dell'Acqua, G. Giussani, P. Lingeri, G. Mantero, O. Ortelli and C. Ponci, with the artistic collaboration of M. Radice and M. Nizzoli for the realization of the images. On the Artist's House on the Lake, see "Gli architetti di Como alla V Triennale", in *Casabella*, no. 66, June 1933, which published the manuscript by G.T. on the house, and "Casa sul lago per l'artista", in *Domus*, no. 70, October 1933. Analytical drawings on the mathematical rules for the plans and elevations are given by H. Weisemann and M. Bhattacharjee, *Casa sul lago per l'artista*, in S. Germer and A. Preiss (eds.), *Giuseppe Terragni 1904–43. Moderne und Faschismus in Italien*, Klimkhardt & Biermann, Munich 1991.

The key feature of the building is certainly the workshop with its 5.8-metre ceiling, in which a narrow bathroom along one side (with a gallery above it) highlights the double height. This space is characterized by the presence of an enormous wall in reinforced glass, curved at the top to become part of the ceiling. Each wall is angled in a specific direction, forming a precise relationship with the surrounding external areas and creating a different layout.

The reinforced glass wall contains a strip of transparent glass that runs along the entire length at eye-level, framing the panorama overlooking the grounds. The vertical wall to the side of the reinforced glass wall in the workshop contains the only non-rectangular element in the entire building: the round window in the bathroom.

The project reveals a multiplicity of styles, prompting the reflection that it is the result of a series of compromises between those who worked on it. It is obvious (from the sketches that have survived) that Terragni worked on the furnishings for the house, designed especially for the Triennale. It was originally conceived as a steel building (one of the requisites of the exhibition was that the projects had to be dismantled), but the house was subsequently built in wood and taken to pieces at the end of the exhibition.

3.3 Horticulturist's House, Rebbio, 1935–37

After a series of long and distressing events, the next project led to the construction of Terragni's first house. At least three very different projects were elaborated over the course of three years before the architect and the client, Amedeo Bianchi, Chairman of the Como Horticultural Union (hence the name given to the house) agreed to construct the last version.

THE FIRST VERSION, 1935 68-69

Documents found only a few years ago have now enabled us to reconstruct the exact sequence of phases in the design process.

This alters what had been the presumed succession of house

ARTIST'S HOLIDAY HOUSE ON THE LAKE, 1933

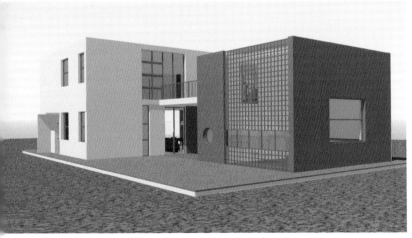

projects[2]. Terragni sketched the first idea for this single-family house while spending the summer of 1935 in the countryside around Como. From these sketches, we can already glimpse the idea of the volume raised up from the ground, originally a sort of bridge. This idea would remain right through to the end, unaffected by all the changes made to the projects.

The first project features an open ground floor, except for the presence of a small service block with an adjoining study, acting as a sort of stairwell that guaranteed the vertical connection between the basement and the second floor. The rectangular area above has a open, linear ground plan, laid out on one floor. The bedrooms stretch along the north wall and the large living-room area is at the opposite end of the corridor. This area runs from one corner to the other of the building shell. It is glassed in from floor to ceiling on three sides, divided by a low, flowing wall, and opens onto a large loggia. From here, you can walk down to the garden and the ground floor, or climb up to the roof garden by means of a daring spiral staircase. The service areas lie at both ends, between the two main areas, along the rear façade broken by the two small loggias. Along the front façade the wall panels are set back from the shell, forming a portico that embellishes the façade with elements of differing depth: projecting and recessed walls, glass panes, *brise-soleils*, railings.

The openings in the four façades (although there are really five, including the roof designed as a roof garden) are differen-

2. The dates 1936–37 indicated in most publications (see the work by Schumacher and Marcianò cit. in the appendix on the subject) should be referred to the construction of the final project in August 1936. Sketches and the vast correspondence between the architect, the client, and the authorities, which was recently found in the AGT in Como, indicate that the initial design should be back-dated to 1935. A preliminary meeting between the architect and the client appears to have taken place in early 1934, through Attilio Terragni. On this long and complex story, see the essay by Annalisa Avon, "La villa del floricoltore a Rebbio (Como) 1936–37", presented at the 1994 conference in Vicenza at the Centro Studi di Architettura di Andrea Palladio, *op.cit.*

tiated depending on their orientation and function: high, narrow slits, long windows, or full-height glass panels covering the space. This clear compositive concept marked a preliminary experimental stage, influenced by European rational architecture; the influence of Le Corbusier's Villa Savoye is clearly recognizable – a purist work par excellence. It is flanked by a refined and innovative structural solution: a metal framework that was technologically advanced, but still avantgarde and little used for residential projects. The project remained on paper, as did the one immediately after it, featuring two apartments created by drastically altering the first version (the ground floor was fully built, in practice thrusting a second body under the raised storey).

THE SECOND VERSION, 1936–37   72-73

Despite his disappointment following the unsuccessful development of the project, Terragni rapidly drew up a new proposal for the villa between June and July 1936. The initial theses underlying the first project, namely, the punctiform loadbearing structure and the suspended volume, were only retained in a structural sense, whereas their qualities were lost.

The doubling of the residential units (at the client's request, the project was to house two families) and the reduced volume (to cut costs) led to a compactness, at the cost of losing the vast open areas, the roof garden and the open plan. The new layout was designed to meet the wishes repeatedly expressed by Amedeo Bianchi in his letters[3].

3. The extensive correspondence (conserved at AGT) between Terragni and the client focused on financial matters and observations regarding the appearance or style of the house are rare. One of the few comments appears in a letter dated 15 June 1936, when A. Bianchi asked the architect "not to be overly stylish, but to create an attractive house in order to draw attention to his [Terragni's] architecture and to my flower garden". The client also expressly wished that the house "should not be affected by common style", but "a virtually square project [...] in order to make the apartment more compact, two floors for two apartments with five rooms each". These excerpts are taken from the essay by Annalisa Avon, *op.cit.*

HORTICULTURIST'S HOUSE, UNBUILT VERSION, 1935

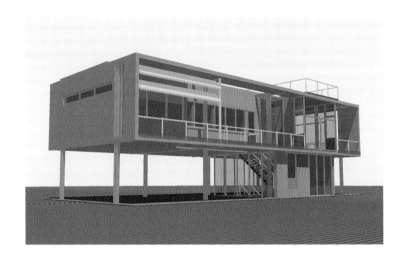

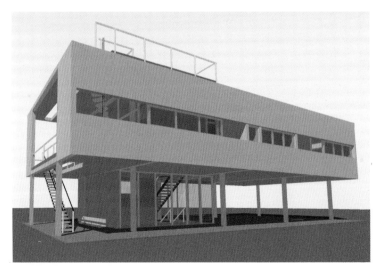

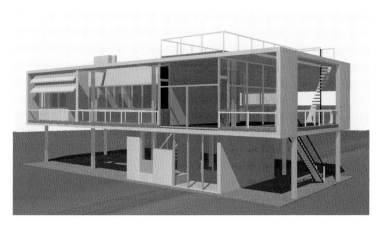

An enormous, unbalanced cornice in open concrete dominates the façade overlooking the street, almost as large as the façade itself, and frames a balcony without even touching it, as if it were a picture. The jutting cornice projects as far out as the outside stair and protects "the outside entrance". You reach the second floor by walking under the giant frame and up the stepped ramp (a typical feature of Terragni's architecture). The second floor entrance is across another balcony, off which a second stair leads up to the third floor, running along the rear façade. This is an ingenious solution to disguise the need for two independent entrances to the two apartments. The façade uses a "mysterious language of rectangles" that, even on the simple, flat façade overlooking the garden, character-ized by horizontal openings, "only acquires richness through the calculation of asymmetry"[4]. To counter this formal self-restraint, the façades overlooking the street are clearly empha-sized by the accumulation of plastic elements: the giant bal-cony, the cantilevered roofs, and the double balcony with out-side stair. The different building elements blend together through mathematical proportions to create a rhythm of forms and colour and a plasticity of volumes and shadows.

Concessions to the client, some of which were stylistically unusual for Terragni (like the gutter running round the roof), were the outcome of numerous revisions of the project. Despite this, the projects for this house should be seen as deci-sive steps in Terragni's stylistic development, refined introduc-tions to the creation of two of the most important projects of Italian rationalism.

76-77 3.4 Villa on the Lake, 1936

We have no information regarding the hypothetical client for this project or the site where it was to be built. The project was first published in the first issue of *Valori Primordiali* in

4. The House for the Horticulturist was first published in "Una Villa di Terragni", in *Domus*, no. 151, May 1941, pp. 12-17, from which this cita-tion is taken; also see M. Piacentini, "Archigrafie architettoniche. Strani avvicinamenti", in *Architettura*, September–October 1941.

February 1938. Work on the design had started already in 1936, probably immediately after the failure of the first project for the Horticulturalist's house. Terragni returned to the compositive principles used in that project and developed them further, turning this into a key project for his research into composition. Through this work, the "most limpid nature of the new architecture", to use Giolli's words[5], would have had an even more decisive influence on contemporary architecture if the work had been built or more widely published.

Only a few, detailed drawings have been preserved of this house – showing its considerable size, approximately 12 metres wide by 35 metres long, and grandiose layout, thus justifying its definition as a "villa" in the traditional sense of the word – which emphasize the architect's enthusiasm and the stylistic clarity he had achieved.

The purist prism of the building is suspended three metres from the ground above a regular grid of slim, circular pillars, set back from the façade on the ground plan. The surfaces surrounding the residential spaces are likewise set back from the main volume, creating a second body that can be read separately. This volume is mainly glassed and creates a sort of house within a house, surrounded by terraces, which spreads freely over the grid of pillars forming a raised level. The freestanding stair also leads up to the main floor from the ground level (beside the service rooms), marking the start of the architectural tour: from the gallery to the patio, then onto the roof, which is laid out as a roof garden. The roof is the fifth façade of the house and, like the first version of the Casa per il Floricoltore, it presents an abstract composition of roof-garden elements. The distribution of the layout, which is also based on the previous project, is enriched by spatial surprises. All connections lead through the fluid space of the gallery. At the far end, the compact group of bedrooms, on a single level overlooked by a patio, forms a separate and rather solid part whose

5. The villa first appeared in the only issue of *Valori Primordiali*, February 1938, together with images of the house in Rebbio, and subsequently in *L'architettura*, no. 153, p. 234.

HORTICULTURIST'S HOUSE, BUILT VERSION, 1937

The subsequent filling in of the ground floor drastically altered the design concept.

windows take the form of sliding glass strips. Double-height ceilings occupy most of the residential volume, but this area is limited by two enormous glass walls overlooking the lake, opening onto a wide hanging and covered terrace, from which a broad stair leads down to the lake below. The building is characterized by the fascinating duality of the two longest façades. The one facing onto the street is marked out by the "aggressive physical nature" of its glass slits and bands running along the wall, broken by vertical spirals and wall recesses. On the contrary, the façade facing the lake has a crystalline transparency, which encloses the living space almost invisibly.

3.5 Villa Bianca, Seveso, 1936–37

Dating from the same year, Angelo Terragni commissioned this project from his cousin in November 1936. The last to be constructed, it was intended to be the main building in a vast complex of houses. A large number of sketches show the design process, and the key characteristics of the final project can already be seen in the earliest drawings: a composition of different rectangles in a balanced horizontal structure. A three-storey, squared, and slightly interred parallelepiped rises up on a rectangular plan measuring 24 metres by 12. Above the basement level containing the service rooms is a raised floor with the living areas, the separate night zone, which includes the patio leading up to the roof garden above. The building is topped by cantilevered roofs. These are suspended above the extension of the structural pillars, thrusting outwards over the surface of the roof. Using this mechanism, Terragni overturns the principle of the box raised up from the ground: here, the box is interred and its structure rises skywards. At the far end of the main block, without infringing the perception of a stereometric body with compact corners, the small studio juts out. Its large window overlooking the street is surrounded by a fragile cornice, which frames it without touching it, suspended in the atmosphere. The façades are mostly full and cut horizontally by long windows. They are embellished by jutting cornices and precise shadows. Terragni also brings them to life through the closed geometry of rectangles and stereometric bodies, the outcome of his "plastic sensitivity". A sensitivity that was also noted by Pagano when he wrote: "In this successful game of chiaroscuro, his fantasy affirms the value of a work of art"[6].

3.6 Abstract Composition Laws and Formal Appearance

The private building projects cover, both thematically and chronologically, a definite period in Terragni's formal investigation during which he developed major concepts regarding the house. In order to analyze this itinerary, we will focus on four houses in chronological order[7], leaving aside the preliminary projects of a preparatory nature. In a process of intellectual decomposition using both structural and formal criteria, themes, and terms emerge that make up the grammar of his continuous research into composition. A direct comparison, using the same scale, reveals the constant categories and abstract laws that guide Terragni's composition. Together with the design methods used, these laws create the appearance of the building and the reciprocal relationship between construction and form. Consequently, this reveals the building's attitude to nature, a relationship which is equally characteristic and significant for the very concept of the house.

3.7 The Model of the Four Villas   79-87

The model used for the comparative analysis of the four houses has a hierarchical structure that was conceived to allow certain groups of design elements to be easily displayed. The idea was to compare Terragni's compositive approach through his projects for houses. The complex process of seeing-under-

6. Pagano's opinion appears in "Villa Bianca a Seveso", in *Costruzioni Casabella*, no.156, December 1940.

7. As emerges from the aforesaid documentation, the first version of the House for the Horticulturist preceded the House on the Lake. The analysis therefore follows chronological order: House for the Horticulturist, first version; House on the Lake; House for the Horticulturist, second version; Villa Bianca, as outlined by A. Saggio, in "Five houses by Giuseppe Terragni", in *Journal of Architectural Education*, September 1992, and subsequently developed in the work by the same author *Villa Bianca. Un capolavoro di trasgressione*, in *Materiali per comprendere Terragni e il suo tempo* cit.

PROJECT FOR THE HOUSE ON THE LAKE, 1936 (image by H. Biele)

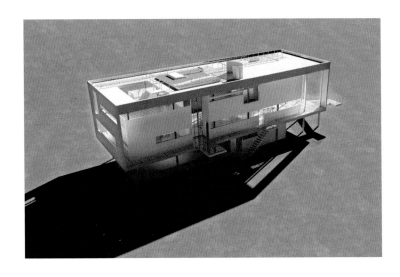

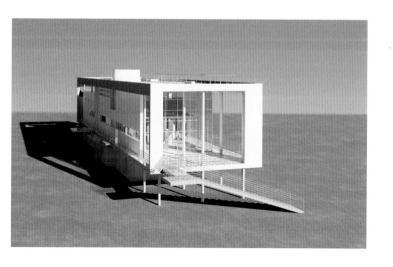

standing-communicating was therefore carried out as elements were gradually added to the structure, starting with the primitive material aspects. However, given that these elements belonged to different composition categories, a series of primitive materials aspects were created for each of these categories: structure, connection to the ground, container, contents, frame, excavated spaces and free elements. Instead of proceeding to construct the model following a subdivision by walls or floors or materials, all the elements belonging to each of the categories were gradually grouped into objects (separately for each house). The models were then completed by assembling these seven objects and adding the elements that could not be allocated to any particular group.

This analytical structure was then displayed using a rendering program, by assigning a colour to the primitive form in the category to be highlighted, and defining a half-transparent material for all the others (likewise primitives, which made the procedure very easy to carry out). This allowed us to create images in which the relationship of the highlighted elements with the finished model is preserved and clearly legible against the semi-transparency of the other elements.

The four houses share the aesthetic appearance of a precise geometric primary form (in line with contemporary European taste that encouraged linguistic simplification in favour of the re-enhancement of stereometric bodies), stemming from the architect's love of rectangular shapes. However, the latter essentially stand out owing to the 3D way of handling the shell. The projects for the first version of the Horticulturist's House and the subsequent House on the Lake reflect Terragni's interest in experimenting with the volumetric approach of purist language, above all Le Corbusier, but in an innovative interpretation: emptying. In the project for the Horticulturist's House, the stereometric longitudinal body, suspended on a grid of set back piloti, illustrates the abstract meaning of the purist composition, which is corroded from all sides and emptied.

This "annulment" of the solid volume has the effect of reducing the façade to a thin cornice, the "frame", which emphasizes the original volume. The "plate"-like head walls (mainly solid

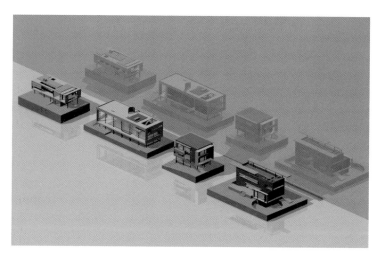

*Projects for the Horticulturist's House (1935), House on the Lake (1936),
Horticulturist's House (1937), Villa Bianca in Seveso (1936–37).*

and still treated in a purist manner with different cuts), "which
cannot be rotated by ninety degrees" (B. Zevi)[8], deny the existence of the full corner as a definition of volume. The frame
motif, with its gigantic dimensions, completely reveals the
internal rules, "the back" becomes the main façade, dense with
depth. Changes in depth define the rooms, offset or superimposed, set back or forwards, blind or transparent, given
rhythm by the play of chiaroscuro. The whole surrounded by
the frame. The initial volume is transformed into a box that
takes on a new role as a macro-container. Terragni tries out the
potential of the container frame in the subsequent project for
the House on the Lake. Defying the technical and expressive
outcome of reinforced concrete, he attains a new, "Michelan-
giolesque" dimension by applying a giant late Renaissance
order in an updated interpretation that reveals the possibility

8. B. Zevi, *Giuseppe Terragni*, Zanichelli, Bologna 1980.

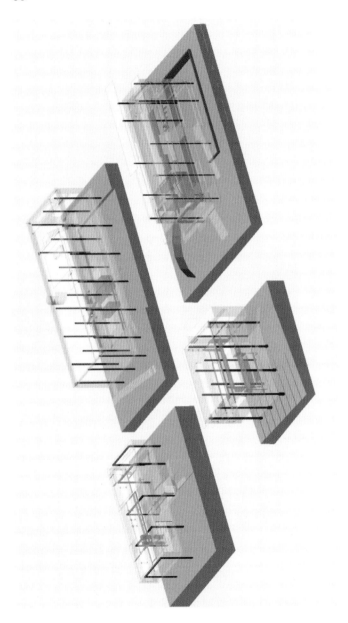

A comparison between four houses: structure.

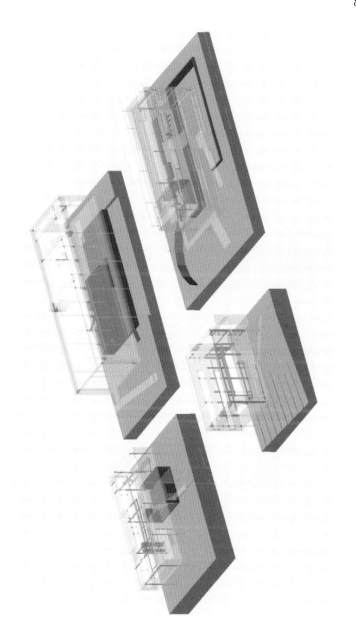

A comparison between four houses: connection.

A comparison between four houses: duality between container-contents.

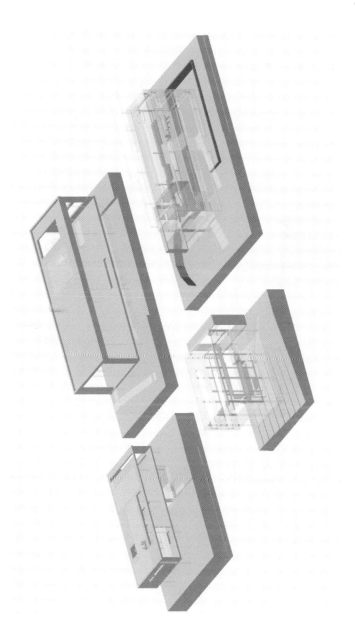

A comparison between four houses: architectural frame.

A comparison between four houses: empty spaces.

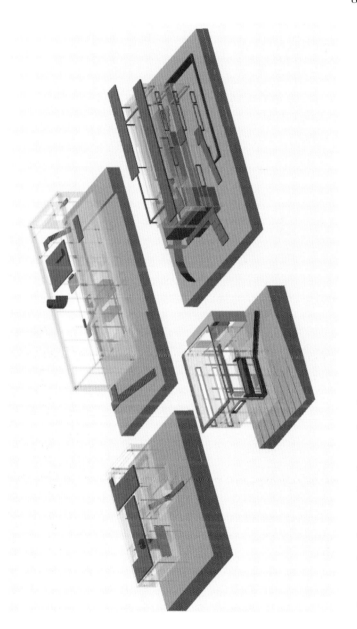

A comparison between four houses: free elements.

for fluid spatial freedom in ground plans and sections. The syntactical relationship of the container-contents type is clarified between the orthogonal joint of the body and the internal spaces (all the panels enclosing the living spaces are set back from the perimeter of the frame, forming a detached and clearly legible content): the volumes of the terrace and the patio are also treated as solids and united by the container-frame. In his restless search for compositive themes, the architect has developed a typical expressive motif in this "frame-like" structure, giving character to the façades through the effect of spatial stratification and emphasizing the depth of the building. In the context of the residential theme, the cornice jutting out to form a loggia is first found in the house designed for the Triennale, in the role of the façade that joins the open, transparent and blind surfaces, giving them rhythm and depth by adding a chiaroscuro effect. Terragni also experimented using the "frame" in other contemporary projects.

We find the clearest expression of the open frame concept in the project for the House on the Lake. Owing to its size and load-bearing function, right at the outset the frame becomes the dominant element in the composition. Later, the influence of the figurative climate of the Thirties would make Terragni abandon the previous concept and return to the solid volume, which undermined the function of the frame. In the second version of the House for the Horticulturist, the smaller frame protrudes outside the volumetric body, becoming an independent plastic element just set apart from the shell. The "unconstrained frame" contributes to the spatial composition, used to alter the aesthetic value of the volume, not by emptying it but enriching it with a "superstructure" around the existing body. This consists of "free" elements which are gradually transferred from within the empty volume to outside it, becoming protrusions of the walls.

The design method is similar to that used in abstract art[9]: the

9. On the influence of abstract art on Terragni's compositions, see F. Fonatti, *Giuseppe Terragni. Poeta del Razionalismo*, in *Architektur und*

principle of the (virtual) "breaking down" of the volume using sliding planes and rectangular volumes, which might also be understood as the doubling of the volume. This operation is first carried out on the plans and is then translated to the elevations (with the new idea of creating two front elevations on the corner): a virtual rectangle becomes a four-dimensional grid, projected into the atmosphere as if it were a shadow projected by a body in a plastic picture. This creates a zone of continuous sliding, depending on both the horizontal and vertical practicability of the living spaces. The dynamic tension of the offset planes is expressed in the third dimension through the lateral shift of the frame and the unbalanced asymmetrical signs of jutting out parts, balconies, ramps and cantilevered roofs. The frame flanks the group of free elements that, by alternating with empty spaces, set the limits of a virtual block in front of the plane of the façade.

In the Villa Bianca, we expect yet another dynamic clash: the volumetric mass, with its formal rigour, compact corners, and mainly solid elevations, is set firmly on the ground with the basement and the prostrate rectangular body of the terrace. This is countered by the free elements, the jutting out elements, the framed glass sections, long ramps and horizontal plates, all rectangular in shape, which create a lively group around the shell and "undermine" the static nature of the block, "moving the masses"[10] involved in the start of the parallel sliding of juxtaposed or superimposed rectangles, both on

Baufachverlag, Wien 1987, pp. 78–91. This discusses an analogy between the abstract compositions by Mario Radice, a close friend of the architect, and Terragni's own design methods, in particular for the "Horticulturist's" House. On the same subject, see also T. Schumacher, *op.cit.*, p. 105.

10. In the previous Villa per il Floricoltore, the unconstrained elements are gathered within the geometric limits of the offset atmospheric volume. By contrast, the autonomous rectangular spaces of Villa Bianca move in an open sliding system, interrelated by tension and forming an intriguing whole, a lively and contradictory "superstructure" to the block, as Mario Labò explains. These quotations are taken from M. Labò, *Giuseppe Terragni*, Il Balcone, Milan 1947, p. 18.

the ground plan and in the elevations. The block is released at the top through the elegant wings, which jut out asymmetrically at opposite corners of the building, as if wishing to break the volume in two directions.

The "frame" undergoes the last stage of its conversion: from a gigantic frame to an "isolated" architectural element, from its primary function of containing to that of framing. Having been released from its role as a unifier of different spaces inside the perimeter of the primary form, it now assumes the role of the disturber. The "antagonist" frame introduces the "front" to the rear volume, creating a second layer of superimposition while sliding. Having been detached in extremis from the façade, it is suspended in a vacuum, held in position by the tall body of the primary volume, which it frames without touching it. The joint interpretation of these two elements make increasingly complex (and we might say poetic) projections, as well as retaining the syntactical relationship of the microcontainer-contents on a drastically reduced scale, whereas the character is transformed into a free element.

3.8 Relations with Nature

Changes in the character of the façade depending on the underlying compositive principles also have repercussions on the building's relationship with its natural surroundings. A house stands out for its privileged natural site, through the motif of the panoramic belvedere. It could also be identified in the concept of the body raised up from the ground or the raised storey, one of Terragni's typical themes, which allows the residents to enjoy the beauty of the view. Moreover, being raised up from the ground and the surrounding countryside, from afar the house looks like a work of art set in green surroundings.

The houses, with giant frames, are opened up through their transparent floors, letting themselves be invaded by nature, integrating a multitude of natural conditions in their flowing spatial layout: the terraces become bridgeheads, loggias, balconies, hanging gardens, and even roofs laid out as roof gardens. All these settings are involved in a vibrating vertical itinerary between exterior and interior, at several levels. Vertical curtain walls weave the volume with air and light. The living spaces of the House on the Lake are never directly exposed to the atmosphere, but only see it through an intermediate, semi-closed zone created between the perimeters of the container and its inhabited contents. Relations with nature are overturned when the building reacquires its volume (in the House for the Horticulturist, second version), hiding its interior with closed walls. In a dialogue between opening and closing, which communicates with the "outside" of its being. Ribbon windows frame "perspective effects" and the "different portions of sky and country". Those elements that have been released from the rigour of a box-like static nature leap into the atmosphere in order to conquer it in every direction, "escaping from the closed form into nature". But the block is still firmly anchored to the ground dug out at different levels. Having been neglected in earlier houses, the ground returns to the fore as an important category in the design process.

The house embodies a dialectic dialogue, opening itself up to the need for light and air and the pleasure of turning the panorama into a sort of dramatic backdrop.

In this architectural climate fuelled by the constant interchange between art, architecture, and literature and an unprejudiced opening up to European ways of thinking, as well as the Mediterranean culture (only this can account for the surprising vivacity of Villa Bianca), Terragni focuses his interests on searching for the primary form. By integrating, contaminating and transforming all these influences through the development of house projects, he investigates two strategies for fighting against the traditional static and compact volume, attaining a level of poetic expression that surpasses geometric definition.

Further reading

Two themes are explored in parallel throughout this work: on the one hand, Terragni and his design activities, and on the other, the computer, or rather the possibilities of using information technology techniques for the study, analysis, and criticism of architecture. For specific publications on Giuseppe Terragni, readers should refer to the individual chapters, which list the main studies on the architect from Como. On the subject of virtual reality, it is particularly worth noting the work by Tomas Maldonado, *Reale e virtuale*, Feltrinelli, Milan 1992. Maldonado guides the reader through the problems of the simulation of reality, the cognitive power of images, the relationship between the model, representations, and reality, paying special attention to the implications linked to the development of IT.

THE MEANING OF HISTORICAL RESEARCH

There is a vast compendium of studies on Terragni and his work, but it is important to cite a few key publications. First and foremost, the special issue "Omaggio a Terragni" in *L'architettura – cronache e storia*, no. 153, July 1968, published to coincide with a conference organized in Como by Bruno Zevi, who first presented an extensive iconographic catalogue to Terragni's architectural works, marking the twenty-fifth anniversary of his death. The next issue, "L'eredità di Terragni e l'architettura italiana", in *L'architettura – cronache e storia*, no. 163, May 1969, contained the proceedings of the Como conference. Some time later, Ada Francesca Marcianò completed *Giuseppe Terragni. Opera completa. 1925–1943*, Officina, Rome 1987. This work was the first to classify Terragni's architecture into different themes, accompanied by many previously unpublished drawings preserved in the Como archive. Thomas Schumacher's *Surface and Symbol. Giuseppe Terragni and the Architecture of Italian Rationalism*, Princeton Architectural Press, New York 1991, appeared in 1991. Recently, Antonino Saggio has published *Giuseppe Terragni. Vita e opere*, Laterza, Bari 1995, which continues a series of earlier studies on Terragni at greater depth. Some images in this book were generated by the research outlined in earlier chapters. The conference in Vicenza organized in 1994 by the "Centro Studi di Architettura Andrea Palladio" and the "Fondazione Giuseppe Terragni", which runs the Como Archive, was followed by the publication of *Giuseppe Terragni. Opera completa* (edited by Giorgio Ciucci), Electa, Milan 1996. This brings together the contributions submitted by many researchers who attended the conference, gives a chronological order to Terragni's works, introduces the archive material, and provides an extensive bibliography.

1. THE ROLE OF THE COMPUTER

1.1 A Growing Presence

On the subject of the development of computer techniques, see *Computergestützter Architekturmodellbau* by Bernd Streich and Wolfgang Weisenberger, published by Birkhäuser, Basel 1996, which gives a systematic analysis of the development of

CAAD (Computer Aided Architectural Design) and its various possible uses at a professional level. The text is accompanied by an extensive technical bibliography. On the researcher's role and the countless problems linked to research methodology, a collection of essays and articles by André Corboz has recently been published: *Ordine sparso. Saggi sull'arte, il metodo, la città e il territorio*, Franco Angeli, Milan 1998.

1.2 Structuring Data

The concept of structure can be analyzed further, in its various forms, in Kurt Bauknecht and Carl August Zehnder, *Grundzüge der Datenverarbeitung*, Teubner, Stuttgart 1985, and Carl August Zehnder, *Informationssysteme und Datenbanken*, Vdf, Zürich 1989, which focus attention on the different possible structures for data banks, including the hierarchical one illustrated later in this book.

1.3 Simulation and the Model

On the subject of models, editing, and tools, see the book by Gerhard Schmitt, *Architectura et Machina. Computer Aided Architectural Design und Virtuelle Architektur*, Vieweg, Wiesbaden 1993. This provides a comprehensive illustration of the problems linked to the use of simulation in architecture, presenting numerous examples of tools, the possible use of models, and other interesting problems linked to the grammar of form and the use of project prototypes. By the same author, see *Architektur mit dem Computer*, Vieweg, Braunschweig 1996, which is more schematic but has an extensive glossary.

1.4 Hierarchical Structures

On the concept of hierarchical structures and their semantic potential, see the following articles by Antonino Saggio: "Die Logik der Simulation. Wiederaufbau, kritische Analyse und Renovation von Bauten der Architekturmoderne mit Hilfe des Computers", in *Architese*, January 1994; *Rekonstruktion und Analyse der Architektur Giuseppe Terragnis*, in Gerhard Schmitt, *Architectura et Machina* cit.; *Hypertext, Solid Modelling and Hierarchical Structures in Architectural Formal Analysis*, in *Caad Futures 1993*, North-Holland, New York 1993, p. 289-309; "Strutture gerarchiche nella ricostruzione e nell'analisi critica dell'architettura", in *Archimedia*, n. 2, March/April 1994. See also Vincent Pierret, *Interprétations de l'oeuvre architecturale de Terragni*, cap. 4, "Analyse par A. Saggio", relatore V. Brunetta, ISACF La Cambre, Bruxelles 1997.

2. COMMEMORATIVE PROJECTS

2.1 Materials

A large proportion of Terragni's surviving iconographic material is preserved in the archive of the Fondazione Giuseppe Terragni in Como. It has been published in parts in the monographs cited earlier. The archive also contains a large number of personal documents and letters, which are important to establish relationships between the architect and clients or authorities, as well as the precise chronology of the projects. To date, these documents have only been partially studied. On Gruppo 7 and the theories expressed, see the series of four articles written and published by the Group in *La Rassegna Italiana*, nos. 103, 105, 106 and 108. These articles have been published repeatedly and can be found in the book edited by M. Cennano, *Materiali per l'analisi dell'architettura moderna. La prima esposizione italiana di Architettura Razionale*, Fiorentino, Naples 1973. This quotation is taken from the fourth article, appropriately titled "Una nuova epoca arcaica". On Carlo Giulio Argan's opinion of the meaning of these contradictions between antique-modern and futurism-metaphysics, see his paper in the proceedings for the conference *L'eredità di Terragni e l'architettura moderna*, published in issue 163 of *L'architettura – cronache e storia*, from which the excerpt in the text is also taken. On the traditional cultural positions and relations with Ojetti, see the chapter by Ellen R. Shapiro, *Ojetti e Terragni: classicismo, razionalismo e fascismo*, in G. Ciucci (ed.) *Giuseppe Terragni. Opera completa* cit., which introduces the figure of the intransigent art historian and the artistic and cultural problems of the time.

2.2 Strategies and the Structure of Models
On the concept of the computer as interlocutor, and the link between reconstructive strategy and hierarchical structure, see the articles by Saggio already mentioned in 1.4.

2.3 Understanding the Projects
The project by Federico Frigerio, which inspired that by Terragni and Lingeri, even if they then altered their intentions, is presented in F. Frigerio (ed.), *Per il monumento ai caduti*, Como 1923, and in F. Frigerio (ed.), *Progetto per un monumento ai 620 caduti in guerra della città di Como nella torre comunale del Broletto*, Como 1923. The events surrounding the competition were reported in the daily papers for 1926: *Il secolo d'Italia* and *La Provincia di Como*, and also in *Catalogo per la Mostra dei bozzetti nel palazzo del Broletto*, a booklet produced by the Committee for the commemoration of the war victims from Como, Como 1925. These publications are summarized by Giudo Zucconi in G. Ciucci (ed.), *Giuseppe Terragni. Opera completa* cit. On the subject of the Land Reclamation monument and the circumstances surrounding reclamation operations, the book by Riccardo Mariani, *Fascismo e città nuove d'Italia*, Feltrinelli, Milan 1976, perhaps presents the fullest description of the historical events linked to Mussolini's land reclamations. On the monument itself, see Pietro Maria Bardi, "Nota informativa", in *L'Ambrosiano*, 25 March 1932; also the letter from Terragni to Margherita Sarfatti *Risposta alle osservazioni di un critico d'arte*, cited in no. 153 of *L'architettura – cronache e storia*. In this letter, the architect describes the monument and comments on it at length. In his description, Terragni does not include the base of the monument as an element in the composition; however, from the photos of the model preserved in the archives of the Giuseppe Terragni Foundation, it cannot be regarded as anything else.

2.4 Hypothesis of Reality
The project for a cathedral in reinforced concrete appeared for the first time in *Architettura*, X, May 1932, in an article illustrating the Exhibition of Rationalist Architecture in Florence that also described the project. A letter from Terragni to Pietro Bardi dated 17 February 1932 is preserved in the archive of the Giuseppe Terragni Foundation and which clarifies the intentions of the project: to demon-

strate the suitable nature of reinforced concrete in the construction of religious and commemorative buildings. Among the drawings preserved in Como are at least two variants of the project, regarding the way the space in front of the church was handled. The first solution, which is drawn in greater detail and has a narthex opposite the body of the church, has been used for the computerized reconstruction; the other does not have a narthex, but the stairway is inserted between the bell-towers and there is a vast space in front of the main entrance.

2.5 To Roberto Sarfatti, 1932–35

Margherita Sarfatti was recently the subject of a book by P.V. Cannistraro and B.R. Sullivan, *The Duce's Other Woman*, New York 1993. This is the most complete biography of Sarfatti and also describes the events leading up to the monument to her son who died in the First World War. On the project, it is important to note that a letter from Sarfatti to Terragni, preserved in the Como archive, gives crucial evidence for dating the monument. In this letter, dated 12 March 1932, Sarfatti expresses an unequivocal opinion regarding a project for the monument that Terragni has already shown her. She criticizes it as being "…too accidental and symmetrical, as if in play…". The letter not only shows that Terragni was working on the project in 1932, but that he started to work on a very free composition, namely the first version, gradually reducing the number of elements and their complex relationships. This contradicts the thesis put forward by some experts, who believe that the free solutions represented "fall-back solutions" when the project had reached a much later stage. The Sarfatti project was therefore contemporary to the project for the Cathedral and the Land Reclamation monument, on which Margherita Sarfatti also commented in the same letter.

3. TERRAGNI'S VILLAS: A PORTFOLIO AND AN ANALYSIS

3.1 Terragni and the Composition Theme of the House

On the subject of the house in modern architecture, the most original work is perhaps that by F.R.S. York, *The Modern House*, Architectural Press, London 1934, which illustrates the most avantgarde houses of the time. A recent publication, *Materiali per comprendere Terragni e il suo tempo*, vol. II, edited by A. Artioli and G.C. Borellini, BetaGamma Editrice, Viterbo 1996, contains several articles on the architect from Como. A one-day seminar on Terragni was held in November 1993 in Milan "to remember the great architect on the fiftieth anniversary of his early death". Precise descriptions of the projects examined here are given in Ada Francesca Marcianò, *op.cit.*, and the articles by Antonino Saggio mentioned earlier, above all the chapter "Oltre il Razionalismo". On the theme of formal appearance in Terragni's work, see F. Mariano (ed.) *Terragni. Poesia della razionalità*, Istituto Mides, Rome 1983, and the chapter by T. Schumacher, "Terragni and his sources: ancient and modern", in *The Danteum*, Triangle Architectural Publishing, New York 1985, p. 61–87. By the same author see *Surface and Symbol* cit. which presents materials and interpretations regarding the various influences on Terragni (p. 96–106 and 240–246).

The Information Technology Revolution in Architecture is a new series reflecting on the effects the virtual dimension is having on architects and architecture in general. Each volume will examine a single topic, highlighting the essential aspects and exploring their relevance for the architects of today.

Series edited by **Antonino Saggio**

Other titles in this series:

Information Architecture
Basis and future of CAAD
Gerhard Schmitt
ISBN 3-7643-6092-5

HyperArchitecture
Spaces in the Electronic Age
Luigi Prestinenza Puglisi
ISBN 3-7643-6093-3

Digital Eisenman
An Office of the Electronic Era
Luca Galofaro
ISBN 3-7643-6094-1

Digital Stories
The Poetics of Communication
Maia Engeli
ISBN 3-7643-6175-1

Natural Born CAADesigners
Young American Architects
Christian Pongratz / Maria Rita Perbellini
ISBN 3-7643-6246-4

For our free catalog please contact:

Birkhäuser – Publishers for Architecture
P. O. Box 133, CH-4010 Basel, Switzerland
Tel. ++41-(0)61-205 07 07; Fax ++41-(0)61-205 07 92
e-mail: sales@birkhauser.ch
http://www.birkhauser.ch